Mark Twain Memorial, Hartford, Conn.

Mark Twain

The Story of Samuel Clemens

by Jim Hargrove

 CHILDRENS PRESS, CHICAGO

Specified extracts from THE AUTOBIOGRAPHY OF MARK TWAIN
Edited by Charles Neider
Copyright © 1959 by The Mark Twain Company
Copyright © 1959 by Charles Neider
By permission of Harper & Row, Publishers, Inc.

Library of Congress Cataloging in Publication Data

Hargrove, Jim.
  Mark Twain: the story of Samuel Clemens.

  Includes index.
    1. Twain, Mark, 1835-1910—Biography—Juvenile
literature. 2. Authors, American—19th century—
Biography—Juvenile literature. 3. Humorists, American—
Biography—Juvenile literature. I. Title.
PS1331.H28   1984   818'.409 [B]   83-23157
ISBN 0-516-03204-6

1 2 3 4 5 6 7 8 9 10 R 93 92 91 90 89 88 87 86 85 84

Table of Contents

Chapter 1

THE GANG FROM HANNIBAL

In the 1840s, many of the schoolchildren in Hannibal, Missouri, believed that Holliday's Hill was the highest mountain in the world. It just had to be Holliday's Hill, unless it was Lover's Leap just a few miles south across town. Hannibal was nestled right between the two mountains, on the western bank of the Mississippi River. Nearly everyone believed that Holliday's Hill, rising nearly three hundred feet above the Mississippi, must be one of the world's great peaks.

One of the true believers was a barefoot boy of twelve named Sam Clemens. Young Sam was well known to the parents of Hannibal. In fact, his behavior had been noticed—if not praised—by nearly every adult in the town. It wasn't so much that he had smoked a corncob pipe since the age of nine. It wasn't so much that he cussed a bit and got into fights every so often. It was more *his entire way of life* that worried the peaceful residents of Hannibal.

Had he thought about it, this widespread attitude might have struck Sam as a strange one indeed. He was, after all, an explorer and an adventurer. Now and then, a few things would go wrong, but a mishap or two was surely a part of every great adventure. And it was adventure that brought him and three schoolmates to the top of Holliday's Hill during the warm months of 1847.

Since long before any of the townsfolk could remember, a huge boulder was perched delicately near the top of the hill. As far as anyone knew, the great rock had been part of the scenery along the river north of Hannibal since the town had been terrorized by Indian raids. Everyone may well have thought that the boulder would fall some day. No one, except Sam and his three friends, could say just when.

The four boys had studied the rock for many months. They were so serious in this study that they had to play hooky from school several times in order to examine the boulder up close. They guessed that it weighed at least 300 million pounds. More important, they decided that the giant stone had stayed in the same place for too long.

But which way should they move it? By raising the rock just a few feet, Sam reasoned, it could be placed at the very top of Holliday's Hill. On the other hand, he thought, by moving it just a few inches down, the boulder might well continue moving on its own. It was on this latter plan that the schoolmates settled.

Three of the four boys began their furious work. Only Sam did little or no digging. He sat alone at the top of the hill. From that higher point, he could examine the rock from a different angle and give suggestions about the digging. He could also be on the lookout for anyone who might come along to waste their time by asking silly questions.

Saturday marked the fourth day of the great effort. By now, small mountains of dirt were piled on two sides of the giant boulder. The teetering rock showed that the project was nearly finished.

"Hold it, men!" Sam shouted suddenly. "Don't let 'er go a-leanin' no more." From his lookout point, he had spotted a group of picnickers near the foot of the hill. "We'll have to wait for these stragglers to pass." While his three friends struggled to hold the great boulder steady, Sam studied the view far below him as he waited.

Years later, writing under his famous pen name of Mark Twain, Sam described what happened next. "I remembered how we sat down, then, and wiped the perspiration away, and waited to let a picnic party get out of the way in the road below—and then we started the boulder. It was splendid. It went crashing down the hillside, tearing up saplings, mowing bushes down like grass, ripping and crushing and smashing everything in its path. . . ."

Reaching the foot of Holliday's Hill at breakneck speed, the boulder struck a woodpile and broke it into splinters. Springing high into the air, it sailed over a horse-drawn cart as the Negro slave driving it watched in terror. Finally, it completely demolished a small barrel-making shop. As fate would have it, the shop had been built on the exact spot the boulder chose as its final resting place. Sam thought that it would be many a year before man or beast would try to move that massive rock again.

But it wouldn't take long for the deed to be noticed. Some workers from the barrel shop were already starting to climb the hill to investigate. The boys barely had time to congratulate one another. Then they hightailed it in the opposite direction for the safer ground of Hannibal.

It was pranks such as this, and dozens of others, that convinced the townsfolk that young Sam Clemens would never amount to anything. They couldn't have been more wrong. In his long and rich lifetime, Sam would write more than thirty-five books. Among them would be some of the most famous works by any American writer, including *The Adventures of Tom Sawyer* and *The Adventures of Huckleberry Finn*. He would write thousands of newspaper and magazine articles. Several times he would travel throughout much of the world giving speeches to large audiences crowded together to hear the famous American writer speak.

Like the characters he wrote about, Sam's life was filled with adventure and daring. He would have exciting experiences as a soldier, a Mississippi riverboat pilot, and a prospector. In his many travels he would see the United States from the Atlantic to the Pacific and cross oceans to see the world. He would even walk into the fiery interior of a volcano in Hawaii, and he would climb to the top of yet another one in Europe. But in all his adventures, even as an old man traveling the world to talk about his famous books, the spirit of a young boy from Hannibal, Missouri, seemed to move restlessly inside him.

Sam was born in the tiny village of Florida, Missouri, on November 30, 1835. At the time of his birth, people all over the world had been amazed by the appearance of Halley's Comet in the night sky. This well-known comet, looking like a bright ball of light with a long, fiery tail, visits the earth only once every seventy-six years.

Late in his life, Sam said that he would live until Halley's Comet returned. He passed away in his seventy-sixth year in April of 1910, when the comet was once more lighting up the night sky. It would not return again until 1986.

At the time of Sam's birth, Andrew Jackson was president of the United States. Abraham Lincoln, twenty-five years shy of becoming the sixteenth president, had just lost his fiancee, Ann Rutledge.

Americans by the thousands were heading west. They were following the promise of open land, plentiful game for food, and the opportunity of finding a new and better way of life in the West. By the 1830s, a handful of brave pioneers had already crossed the continent to arrive at the Pacific Coast. But for most Americans, Missouri was part of the far western frontier.

A few years earlier Sam's father, John Marshall Clemens, had been part of the rush west. He had moved from Virginia to Missouri by way of Kentucky and Tennessee. Throughout his life, John Clemens was a hardworking man, respected everywhere he lived. By the age of twenty-three, he had become a lawyer. He would later serve as a justice of the peace.

Despite his hard work and honesty, John was often very poor. Few people in the American frontier had money to hire a lawyer. Arguments usually were settled in other ways. At times he would hold odd jobs as a clerk, but the wages were low. In several of the towns where he lived he opened small general stores, but he was not a sharp businessman. Profits, if any, were tiny.

John Clemens met Jane Lampton, a native of Kentucky who would become Sam's mother, in 1823. They were married the same year. Although Jane had another boyfriend at the time, the pair had not been getting along. Jane agreed to marry John Clemens partly out of anger at her former boyfriend.

Settling in Jamestown, Tennessee, the couple had four children. They were named Orion, Pamela, Margaret, and Benjamin. Sam had not yet been born.

Although they were poor, the family did manage to buy one prized possession. Probably around 1827, in a rare moment with cash at hand, John bought a huge tract of land near Jamestown. At a cost of four hundred dollars, the land included somewhere between 75,000 and 100,000 acres of forests and rolling hills.

John Clemens held the title to the land for twenty years until his death. Every year, he somehow managed to pay the taxes on it, which averaged about five dollars annually.

The land never brought a fortune to the Clemens family. But in good times and bad, mostly bad, the family took much comfort in knowing that it was the proud owner of 100,000 acres of prime timberland in the Cumberland Mountains of Tennessee.

In the early 1830s, the young nation was in the grip of a serious depression. Nearly everyone found money hard to come by. Never wealthy and with a rapidly growing family, John and Jane Clemens now found it almost impossible to make ends meet. Both parents felt that they needed to move in order to make a fresh start. Jane's sister would help considerably in that decision.

Some years earlier, Jane's sister Patsy had married a man named John Quarles. John and Patsy Quarles lived on a five-hundred-acre farm a few miles from Florida in neighboring Missouri. The Quarles family must have been fairly wealthy. Besides being able to raise eight children, they owned fifteen or twenty Negro slaves.

Realizing that the Clemens family was in trouble, John

and Patsy invited them all to come to Florida. In the early spring of 1835 Jane and John Clemens, their four children, and a slave girl named Jennie, moved to the Missouri town where the Quarles family lived. Jane would soon be pregnant with the child that would become known throughout the world as Mark Twain.

Sam was born two months early, in November. He had a tiny body and an unusually large head. As a baby, he was weak and sickly. During the earliest years of his life, Jane feared that he wasn't strong enough to reach another birthday. The hard life of the frontier offered his mother plenty of good reasons to be so worried. A dozen years after Sam was born, the *Hannibal Gazette* newspaper summed up the odds for reaching old age in the American West. "One quarter of the children born, die before they are one year old; one half die before they are twenty-one, and not one quarter reach the age of forty."

For more than the first decade of his life, Sam's worried mother poured medicines into her young son. The cures included pills, tonics, health baths, poultices, and castor oil by the barrelful. Sickness was a constant worry. Before Sam reached the age of ten, his sister Margaret and his brother Benjamin would both die from childhood diseases.

To his mother's great surprise, Sam continued to live, although he never seemed very strong or healthy. His early years were troubled by frequent sleepwalking. Rising from bed while still soundly asleep, he would often wander throughout the small Florida house. When awakened by a voice or a tap on the shoulder, he would fall to the floor in a heap. Still, his mother considered it a miracle that her young boy kept on living and growing.

If Sam's fortunes seemed to be improving, his father's were not. Once again, John and the family were discovering that yet another town was failing to live up to its promise of prosperity for all. The tiny village of Florida had been built on the banks of the Salt River. The little Salt River was not large enough to carry sizable boats, and the Mississippi River was many miles away. Farmers who wished to sell their goods out of town had to carry them overland in horse-drawn carts. In Florida, it was difficult for anyone to earn much of a living.

On the other hand, towns along the Mississippi River were growing rapidly. From Minnesota to New Orleans the mighty Mississippi was fast becoming the highway of the West. Southern plantation owners used the river to ship huge cargoes of cotton, tobacco, and molasses northward. Northerners sent their grain, livestock, and manufactured goods south. Towns along the watery route were booming, even in the hard economic times of the late 1830s.

In November, 1839, soon after the death of Sam's sister Margaret at the age of nine, John and Jane Clemens moved their family to Hannibal, Missouri. On the western bank of the Mississippi some thirty miles from Florida, Hannibal was already enjoying the benefits of a river town.

John Clemens sold his land in Florida and traded it for a quarter of a city block in downtown Hannibal. Figuring that the land would still be worth a fortune to his children, he managed to hold on to the 100,000 acres in Tennessee.

Sam was nearly five years old and ready to start his schooling. More than half a century later, he wrote about his life in a book he called the *Autobiography of Mark Twain*. In his own words, here is how Sam remembered that first day at school:

"My school days began when I was four years and a half old. There were no public schools in Missouri in those days but there were two private schools—terms twenty-five cents per week per pupil and collect it if you can. Mrs. Horr taught the children in a small log house at the southern end of Main Street. Mr. Sam Cross taught the young people of larger growth in a frame schoolhouse on the hill. I was sent to Mrs. Horr's school and I remember my first day in that little log house with perfect clearness, after these sixty-five years and upwards—at least I remember an episode of that first day. I broke one of the rules and was warned not to do it again and was told that the penalty for a second breach was a whipping. I presently broke the rule again and Mrs. Horr told me to go out and find a switch and fetch it."

Sam was glad that he had been given the job of finding the

switch. He was sure that he could find just the right one. Buried in the mud, he found a thin shaving of wood left by some barrelmakers. Even though the wooden switch was soft and rotten, he was sure that it was just right for him.

He brought the rotten piece of wood back to his teacher and tried his best to look sad and pitiful. But things didn't go as he had hoped. The teacher looked at him crossly and called him by his full name, Samuel Langhorne Clemens. Once again in his own words, Sam told about his earliest lesson in school:

"I was to learn later that when a teacher calls a boy by his full name it means trouble. She said that she would try and appoint a boy with better judgment than mine in the matter of switches, and it saddens me yet to remember how many faces lighted up with the hope of getting that appointment. Jim Dunlop got it and when he returned with the switch of his choice I recognized that he was an expert."

From the low point of that very first day, Sam's opinion of school never got much higher. But in the summer of his seventh year he had the first of a series of vacations that were to be among the happiest experiences of his life.

Uncle John and Aunt Patsy Quarles were still living on the farm near Florida. The farm was just a few miles from where Sam was born. For about five years, Sam made a series of lengthy visits every summer to the Quarles farm.

He would never forget the mouth watering meals served in the large log house on the five-hundred-acre farm. He remembered the fresh venison, wild turkey, fried chicken, rabbits, birds, and squirrel. In the summer, corn, butter beans, and succotash were always fresh. For dessert there was a hot fruit pie or apple dumplings or peach cobbler. Years later, Sam would claim that no one in the North knew how to cook properly.

The farmhouse was surrounded by a large yard. Behind it was a smokehouse for curing meats. Beyond that was an orchard, housing for the slaves, and tobacco fields. Near a small stream that crossed the farm were barns for livestock, a corncrib, horse stables, and a cabin for drying tobacco leaves.

The area of the country near the Quarles farm had always had more than its share of snakes. Sam and his cousins enjoyed finding them along the country road that ran past the farmhouse. They killed poisonous rattlers and the scary-looking puff adders. As did all the schoolchildren in the area, they wrongly believed that one kind of snake could form a loop by biting its tail and roll after people faster than a horse could run. They fled in terror when they thought they had spotted the dreaded "hoop snake."

The children liked to play with the snakes they called "garters" and "house snakes." They especially liked to bring them back to the house, alive and wriggling, and hide them in Aunt Patsy's sewing basket for a surprise. Aunt Patsy was never much amused. Sam was so impressed by the fun of it that he even practiced the trick back in Hannibal. Like her sister Patsy, Jane Clemens was prejudiced against snakes. When he was a grown writer, Sam made fun of ladies who would "jump out of their stockings" when a snake merely "dropped on their shoulders."

Of the many pleasures on the Quarles farm, the one that Sam cherished most was his daily visit to the slave quarters behind the orchard. Most white owners would not let their Negro slaves learn to read or write. The group of fifteen or twenty slaves then living on the farm entertained themselves by reciting and listening to long stories. More than anywhere else, it was probably with the slaves on the farm that Sam learned the gift of storytelling.

By summer's end, Sam had always returned to Hannibal and the school he disliked so much. Teachers at the time seemed to believe that children learned best by memorizing endless passages from books. For a boy like Sam, who spent his young life fleeing from boredom, the method was less than satisfactory. Fortunately, the area around Hannibal, especially along the Mississippi River, held plenty of possibilities for adventure outside of the classroom.

During the warm months, Sam and some of his gang would swim in the Mississippi, exploring its steep banks, or in nearby Bear Creek. Before he was very old, he was mak-

19

ing and "borrowing" all kinds of makeshift rafts to sail on the mile-wide river. The boys swam and fished and played pirates on the river and dug for buried treasure along its shore. They camped out on islands dotting midway between Hannibal and the Illinois shore to the east. In winter they skated on the dark, almost black, ice that formed on the river.

Along the banks of the river south of Lover's Leap was a long, winding cave that many people from around Hannibal enjoyed exploring. The cave was a maze of crooked passageways. It was always possible for explorers to get lost in it. A few years later a town drunkard called Injun Joe wandered into the cave and was lost for days. He survived, he said, by eating bats that lived within the darkened walls. When Sam and his friends explored the cave, they trailed kite string behind them to show the way out.

Of all the enchantments along the river, the greatest were the magnificent steamships. Most would dock briefly at Hannibal before paddling on to the north or south. The *Hannibal Gazette* reported that more than a thousand steamers had visited the town in a single year. Passengers from the ships would tell Sam tales about the great city of St. Louis and the even more magical New Orleans. He was in awe of the proud riverboat pilots who, dressed in fancy clothes and treated like European kings, steered the ships around dangerous obstacles in the river.

When the steamers landed at the Hannibal wharf, large

numbers of passengers would hurry on and off. The huge vessels would be on their way again in a matter of minutes. Black slaves were used to hurry cargo to and from the ships. When the slaves themselves became passengers in the cargo holds, they were often the unhappiest of all the world's travelers.

Sam's life along the Mississippi also had its sorrows. In 1842 his brother Benjamin caught a childhood disease and died at the age of ten. It was the second child John and Jane had seen buried during Sam's young lifetime. The remaining children were Orion and Pamela, both older than Sam, and Henry, his younger brother by two years.

The worried parents' fear of disease would be a lasting one. A few years later, when Sam was ten, Hannibal was struck with an epidemic of measles. Severe cases resulted almost daily in deaths throughout the frightened town. Fearing that he would become infected, Jane forced Sam to stay in the house for week after week. It was a dreary life for the adventurous boy, who was keeping a diary at the time. Day after day, he recorded his dull life: "Got up, washed, went to bed."

Finally, he had had enough. If the measles didn't kill him, the suspense of waiting would. He planned to catch the sickness, live or die, and get the whole thing over. First though, was his daily dose of castor oil.

"Time for your tonic, Samuel," his mother called.

"Already took it, Ma," he lied.

"Samuel Langhorne Clemens," Jane scolded, "you get over here this instant and open your fibbin' mouth!"

After the ordeal, Sam snuck out of the house. His friend Will Bowen was in bed with a bad case of measles. Sam secretly entered the Bowen house, tiptoed into Will's room, and got into bed with his sick friend.

Soon thereafter, Sam came down with a whopping case of the measles. Once again, his parents feared for his life. But both Sam and his friend Will would live a good while longer. Both would live to tumble the huge boulder on Holliday's Hill. And both would live to see their greatest dreams come true, to become pilots of Mississippi riverboats.

During Sam's entire life at home with his parents, the family was poor. Many times it must have been difficult for Jane to put a good meal on the table. Nevertheless, she was always kind to her family, friends, and neighbors. She was even kind to animals. Whenever a stray cat appeared at their doorstep, she always took it in. At one time in 1845, Sam remembered, there were nineteen cats living in their house. That catastrophe made a lasting impression on Sam's father. The father's advice to his daughter Pamela on growing up was to keep a clean house, make her husband feel at home, and not keep too many cats!

John Clemens had been elected justice of the peace in the Hannibal election of 1842. Although the fees he earned were very small, Judge John Marshall Clemens made certain that peace was kept in his Hannibal courtroom. When he was angered by the unruly behavior of a witness in his court, the judge had been known to clobber the man over the head with a hammer.

Judge Clemens in 1846 decided to run for Clerk of the Circuit Court. With that job, he could earn higher wages than those paid to a justice of the peace. By scrimping and saving, he managed to come up with the two dollar fee. He probably could have won the election, but it was not to be.

On March 11, 1847, he traveled to a nearby town for a court case he was personally involved in. On the way home he was caught in a storm of rain, snow, and sleet. As a result of the chilling trip, he was overcome with pneumonia. He died two weeks later, never having reached the age of fifty. On his deathbed, Judge Clemens urged his family to cling to the Tennessee land, which, he still believed, would be worth a fortune. It was the same year that Sam and Will Bowen and two others from the gang would drop that great boulder from Holliday's Hill. Despite the heartaches, there were plenty more great adventures to come.

Chapter 2

GROWING UP ALONG THE MISSISSIPPI

Sam was greatly troubled by his father's death. His sleepwalking became a problem once again. Still worried about the frail health of her son, Jane poured tonics and medicines into him.

Hating the taste of medicine, Sam took every opportunity he could to avoid it. Whenever his mother wasn't looking, he would pour spoonfuls of the wretched stuff between the cracks in the floor. Concerned about the health of plants around the house, he would often give them a healthy dose of the bitter liquids.

In later years, Sam wrote that the worst of all the medicines was a foul brew called Perry Davis's Pain-Killer. Even the offer of a spoonful of the awful medicine made him wish he were dead. One time, he wrote, he was holding a spoonful of the dreaded painkiller when one of the Clemens's cats, Tom, seemed to take a sudden interest in the medication. Thinking that the cat was looking a bit pale, Sam offered it the painkiller. The cat licked the spoon clean and then seemed to go crazy.

Tom arched his back and jumped high into the air. At the same time, the surprised cat made a terrific screech and began bounding throughout the room. In absolute agony, it finally jumped out the window, upsetting all the flowerpots on the sill. With a smirk, Sam thought of how healthy Tom would soon be.

The family now had plenty of other things to worry about. By the same year that John Marshall Clemens died, Jane and her children had become so poor that they no longer could afford to live in their own house. Kindly Hannibal neighbors allowed the family to move in with them.

Without Judge Clemens's wages to help support them, now every member of the family had to help out. Sam's brother Orion was already working in a St. Louis print shop. His sister Pamela was earning tiny fees giving piano lessons to neighborhood children.

Sam's carefree school days were over. For the next several years he would go to classes at Mr. Cross's school only once in a while. Immediately, he had to begin working at odd jobs around town. A delivery boy, a grocer's clerk, a blacksmith's helper, a bookseller's assistant, and a drugstore worker were some of the jobs he held trying to bring money home for the family.

In September the *Hannibal Gazette* advertised for a young man, fourteen or fifteen years old, to work in the office as a printer's helper. The printed advertisement went on to suggest that the boy should be a good reader and live in the country.

Sam lived in the town, not the country, and was two years shy of the required age, but he was a skillful reader and somehow he got the position. Sam became a newspaper apprentice, a young person who works for very low wages in order to learn a new trade. Sam's wages at the *Gazette* were to be room and board (on the days he didn't go home) and two new suits of clothes each year. He would be given, it was agreed, no money whatsoever.

For such mighty wages, there was no shortage of work around the *Gazette*. In the mornings Sam would build a fire for warmth and sweep up the office and haul water from the outdoor pump. Then he would have to clean and oil the printing press and take care of the blank sheets of paper that would become the next edition of the newspaper. On Thursdays, he folded the freshly printed pages and delivered them around town.

Sam worked hard, but even the tiny wages he had been promised by the newspaper owner were difficult to collect. Instead of getting two new suits of clothes, as he had been promised, he got a single hand-me-down that was so big on him that it fit like a circus tent. Even the meals he received left him still hungry for more. He and another apprentice were forced to steal potatoes from the owner's basement and cook them on the sly.

But there were at least a few advantages in Sam's new job. For one thing, he was learning a skill that would be useful to him throughout his life. From the age of twelve on, hardly a year would go by in his long life when the power of the printing press did not figure into his work.

There were other advantages, too. Abraham Lincoln once called the print shop the "poor boy's college." At the *Gazette*, Sam learned much about Hannibal and the world as he helped to prepare each edition of the small newspaper. Part of his job was to read and collect interesting stories from other, larger newspapers from St. Louis and beyond. The best stories would be copied in the *Gazette*. It was not an unreasonable way to learn.

But for Sam the greatest advantage of his job was the time off he got. Although many people who worked in stores and shops had to spend long hours at their trades, the job of newspaper apprentice was a limited one. Sam was usually finished working by three in the afternoon, sometimes much earlier. Those short hours left plenty of time for adventure, pranks, and mischief. And young Sam was seldom at a loss for ideas on those topics.

One warm summer afternoon during his first year at the *Gazette*, Sam had been grounded by the owner for some bit of devilment while the other boys were allowed to go out and play. Alone in the third floor office of the newspaper, Sam had only half of an enormous, ripe watermelon for company. With a great effort he managed to eat all the juicy red fruit without breaking the huge rind that was left over.

So full he could barely move, he sat by the open third floor window and watched the parade of people passing below him on the street. In a town the size of Hannibal, he could recognize most of the people drifting lazily beneath him. But he was most interested in seeing one particular person, his younger brother Henry.

Sam loved everybody in his family, and Henry perhaps most of all, but at times his younger brother could strain his affection. It just didn't seem right for a kid to be so good all the time, and everyone agreed that Henry was as good a boy as they come. He never seemed to get into trouble at school. He never had to make up yarns to explain some bad behavior because he simply never seemed to behave badly. He never even put up a fight about going to Sunday school or church services.

Sam often thought that such perfect behavior was downright unnatural. He got especially angry when his mother would hold up Henry's behavior to him.

"I do declare, Samuel," Jane had said, "if you don't learn a thing or two about proper manners from Henry, you'll be hanged before you're grown." Just thinking about how good Henry was made Sam turn red.

With his face red, Sam sat by the open window and waited for his chance for revenge. Pretty soon, he saw his big opportunity. Henry was walking down Sam's side of the street and would soon be directly beneath him.

Sam eagerly watched Henry's approach. With both hands, he held the huge melon rind out the window waiting for Henry to arrive at just the right spot. When his younger brother was just a few steps from being directly beneath him, Sam let go of his bomb. Sam remembered later that his timing was "beyond admiration."

Not suspecting a thing, Henry took a few more steps before the melon landed directly on the top of his head, splattering in every direction. He didn't seem to know what hit him, or who, or did he? Sam watched him carefully to see if there was any sign of suspicion. When things like this happened, Henry almost always jumped to the conclusion that Sam was behind them. This time, though, he didn't seem to notice.

For several days, Sam avoided getting too close to his brother. He watched for any sign that would seem to show that Henry knew who had dropped the melon on him. Finally, Sam was convinced that Henry didn't suspect him.

But Henry had only been waiting for the best possible moment to get his revenge. When the right opportunity came, he swung into action by hitting Sam on the head with a cobblestone from the street. The rock raised such a bump on his head that Sam claimed he "had to wear two hats for a time."

The biggest insult was yet to come. Sam used every chance he got to try to get Henry into trouble. With the ugly bump on his head, he ran home for what he thought was a perfect opportunity.

"Look what Henry did to me, Ma," Sam complained, parting his hair to show the big bump. "Did it for no reason, too!"

Jane was not impressed. "It's no matter, Samuel," she said with little interest. "If Henry did it, I'm sure you deserved it."

"But Ma, it weren't nothing I was—"

"Now Samuel," his mother interrupted, "I don't want to hear another word about this. If you didn't do something bad just now to catch that bump from Henry, then you must have done something earlier. And if you didn't do it earlier, then you will soon enough. Let this be a lesson to you. I think Henry has found the only way there is to get a point through that thick head of yours."

Life with Henry was like that, and Sam was pretty disappointed. His mother's words stung more than Henry's rock. Do you think Sam learned a lesson about good behavior from his younger brother? Well, if he did, it didn't last very long.

The following winter, Sam and a young friend named Tom Nash decided to go ice skating on the frozen Mississippi River. It was already late in the evening when they had their inspiration. Normally, neither one of the boys would be much interested in skating in the dark. But since neither had bothered to get permission, the outing took on more of the flavor of a real adventure.

By midnight, the two skaters were on the middle of the

river, halfway between the Missouri and Illinois shores. In either direction, it was a half mile to solid ground. The sky was pitch black.

Suddenly, they heard a loud rumbling sound behind them. That sound was followed by a series of sharp cracking noises that broke the silence of the night air. The icy surface of the river was breaking up!

Both skaters knew that in an instant they could be swimming for their lives in the freezing water. So far from land, they would certainly freeze or be crushed to death between giant cakes of ice. Worse yet, the river's current might pull them under a solid sheet of ice where they would die trying to fight their way back to the surface.

Badly frightened, the two boys began skating at top speed toward the Missouri shore. But they started too late. When the moon came out from behind some thick clouds, they could see that there were already open stretches of water between them and the land. In near darkness, they waited until a huge sheet of ice floated into the space of open water in front of them. Then, practically crying from fright, the boys leaped onto the floating ice cake and continued toward shore.

Whenever the moon disappeared behind a cloud it became too dark to see, and the boys had to stop. Whenever they came upon open water they had to wait for the current to push a sheet of ice into their path so that they could continue.

31

It took more than an hour for them to get near the Missouri shore.

Within a stone's throw of safety, one last area of open water stretched out before them. All around the ice was cracking and shifting, sending out a deafening roar as it splintered and piled up ever changing mountains along the shore. Too scared to be sensible, the boys started for the land too soon, leaping from ice cake to ice cake. In the darkness, Tom Nash missed one of the cakes and fell screaming into the river. In the frigid Mississippi, his body would become so cold that he would be unable to move in a matter of minutes.

Fortunately, Tom was close enough to the shore that he could swim just a few strokes and climb up the steep banks to safety. Sam got to the shore just a few seconds later, somehow having escaped the freezing water. Both of the foolish boys survived, but Tom Nash got a chill and was seriously ill for a long time. More than fifty years later, Sam returned to Hannibal for a visit and found his old friend, Tom. Although Tom had become totally deaf, he and the famous writer joked about their foolish days on the frozen Mississippi.

Jane Clemens did her best to keep her children safe and well behaved. Sam of course, offered the greatest challenge. Whenever he got into trouble, his mother decided that a little extra church was just what he needed.

Sam held to a somewhat different opinion. He felt that Sunday morning Bible class, followed by a church service that usually lasted about an hour and a half, was plenty of religious training for just about anybody. But when he behaved badly during the week, Jane insisted that he go to another service on Sunday evening.

One of the highlights of Sam's young life also occurred the same year. Have you ever heard of a *mesmerist*? A mesmerist is a person who tries to hypnotize people. Some of the people of Hannibal had never heard of a mesmerist until, in 1850, a man calling himself a mesmerist visited the little city on the Mississippi.

The man stayed for some time, giving shows on a stage inside a building. Admission was twenty-five cents; children and Negroes, half price. Only a handful of people went to the first show, but the tiny audience saw such amazing things that by the next morning the whole town was buzzing. The next show, and every one thereafter, was packed.

Somehow coming up with the money for admission, Sam managed to go to nearly every performance. What he saw was amazing. People he knew from town would get up on stage with the mesmerist and stare at a magic disk held in his hand. Then they would fall sound asleep while sitting straight up in a wooden chair.

But that was just the beginning of the wonders Sam saw. The mesmerist would walk up to a sleeping man and make him open his eyes. He would say, "There is a rattlesnake crawling up your leg," and the sleeping man would jump up in terror, as if he believed a snake were actually there. After they fell asleep by staring at the magic disk, the mesmerist could get people to believe anything!

Before long, Sam was up on the stage with the other volunteers from the town. He stared into the magic disk and tried to feel sleepy. He tried and tried, and the mesmerist urged him to fall asleep. "Your eyelids are getting heavy," he would say. "You are getting sleepy . . . sleepy . . . sleepy."

But Sam was only feeling foolish. While others were being "mesmerized" right and left, he stayed embarrassingly awake. It filled him with anger when a fellow from his own newspaper staff managed to fall asleep and started doing amazing tricks. Sam was certain that he could do much better, if only he could fall into that magical sleep.

By the fourth performance he could stand it no longer. Sitting on stage and feeling wide awake as ever, he stared into the colorfully painted disk and pretended to get sleepy. In an instant, the mesmerist was standing next to him. His heart pounding from the new attention, Sam pretended to nod off into a deep sleep.

The mesmerist opened Sam's eyes and led him around the stage by holding the magic disk in front of him. Hoping that his phony performance would not be discovered, Sam began doing some of the same tricks the others had done. He jumped in terror from make-believe snakes. He passed buckets of water to an imaginary fire. He even kissed invisible girls that the mesmerist said were standing in front of him.

The audience was, once again, amazed. Now that he was sharing in the glory of being "mesmerized," Sam felt a good deal better. No one seemed to realize that he was faking it. But the real test, he knew, was next.

The mesmerist picked up a large pin from a table on the stage and held it up for the audience to behold. "Ladies and gentlemen," he announced, "this young lad is so under the power of mesmerism that he will not feel pain even if I stick this pin deep into his skin."

And he went on to do just that, many times! The pain was awful. Sam held back his tears and turned his face into an iron mask every time a pin was pushed deeper and deeper into him. The audience gasped.

To Sam's amazement, neither the mesmerist nor the audience seemed to realize his trick. Sam was in heaven. He was a hero. But he was determined to become even more of a hero, to outdo everything the others had done. Somehow, even the mesmerist seemed to realize that Sam was ideal for the show. Soon, the tricks became even grander.

"Ladies and gentlemen," the mesmerist shouted, "I will

now astound you even more with the scientific powers of mesmerism. I will make this youngster do whatever I want merely by thinking and concentrating on the act I wish him to perform. I will not say a word to the lad, yet he will do exactly as I wish." Then the mesmerist stood directly behind Sam, closed his eyes, and seemed to concentrate seriously.

For a moment, Sam was terrified. Now he would surely be caught. He closed his eyes and tried to discover what the mesmerist was thinking, but everything was a blank. Starting to panic, Sam realized that in a moment or two everyone would realize that he had faked the whole thing. By morning the whole town would be laughing at him.

In desperation, Sam did the first thing that came to his mind. When he was almost ready to die of embarrassment, he was startled to hear the mesmerist speak up. "As unbelievable as this may seem, people of Hannibal, the lad has done exactly as I willed. Through the scientific powers of mesmerism, our minds are in direct contact!" What luck, Sam thought. But he figured with a sinking heart that it couldn't possibly work again.

To everyone's amazement, especially Sam's, it worked again and again and again. Every time Sam did something, however strange or silly, the mesmerist astounded the audience by stating that it was exactly what he had willed the boy to do.

Sam became the talk of the town. For two more weeks,

only he and the mesmerist appeared on stage. Each show became more amazing than the last, and Sam's feats became increasingly astounding. When a boy who had won a fist fight with Sam a few weeks earlier came to see the show, Sam was ready. As the mesmerist closed his eyes and began to concentrate, Sam raced to a table on the stage, picked up a gun left as a prop, yelled his enemy's name in a horrible rage, and chased him out of the building. The audience roared with laughter. When a few members of the audience would suggest that the whole thing might be some sort of trick, Sam and the mesmerist were somehow able to convince them otherwise.

No one ever discovered Sam's trick. He waited thirty-five years to admit what he had done, and then only to his mother. To his astonishment, she refused to believe that the whole thing had been faked. "I give you my honor," Sam insisted, "a pin was never stuck into me without causing me cruel pain."

"It is thirty-five years," his old mother replied. "I believe you do think that now but I was there and I know better. You never winced."

Despite his endless mischief and search for adventure, life in Hannibal was not all fun and games for Sam. It was still difficult and at times almost impossible to support himself and help his family. The meager rewards he got from working at the *Gazette* (now renamed the *Courier*) were barely enough to keep himself alive, much less help out his mother and Henry and Pamela.

For some time his brother Orion had been working in a St. Louis print shop trying to earn enough wages to be able to send some money back home. In 1850, the same year that Sam was so thoroughly "mesmerized," Orion decided to return to Hannibal and start his own newspaper.

With less than fifty dollars, Orion managed to get his newspaper, which he called the *Western Union*, started. The newspaper did little to add to Orion's fortunes, but Jane was overwhelmed with joy at having all her children back in Hannibal again.

In January of the following year, Orion offered his brother Sam a job on the new paper. He promised to pay a magnificent wage of $3.50 a week. For such a princely amount of money, as well as the opportunity to work with both of his brothers, Orion and Henry, Sam immediately agreed.

Orion was never a smart businessman, and the *Western Union* never made much money. Not once did Sam ever receive the salary he had been promised. The paper was so poor, in fact, that Orion had to set up the printing press at home. He couldn't even afford the luxury of an office.

But there were other advantages. Sam was now sixteen years old and his genius at writing humorous stories was already beginning to show. He wrote story after story for

Orion's newspaper, many of them very entertaining and funny. When he lacked facts, he often made them up. When something happened in town that was newsworthy but not very interesting, Sam "improved" the event to make people laugh.

Sam "improved" so many things in such a humorous way that soon more people began to enjoy reading the *Western Union*. Before long, Orion borrowed five hundred dollars from an old farmer and bought a larger, established newspaper, the *Hannibal Journal*. At the *Journal*, Sam continued his efforts at "improving" the news, and the paper increased a bit in popularity. Economically, things were looking up at last for Jane Clemens and her family. More help came when Sam's sister Pamela married a wealthy businessman from St. Louis.

Orion's *Journal* had a brief but colorful history. Early in 1852, a fire destroyed the office and the entire newspaper had to move to new quarters. Getting to the point where he could find humor in almost anything, Sam wrote a funny story describing what happened. At around the same time, he published his first magazine story in a popular Eastern magazine called *Carpet-Bag*. The magazine was extremely popular in Hannibal. Nearly everyone in town read Sam's story.

The *Journal* became particularly colorful when Orion took short excursions away from Hannibal, leaving Sam in charge. In early 1853, Orion left for a brief stay in St. Louis, leaving Sam with instructions to get out a single edition of the weekly paper. When Orion returned little more than a week later, he found three people threatening to kill his younger brother because of stories Sam had written in the paper about them. Throughout his life, Sam was a master at attracting attention, both good and not so good.

In the same year, a tragedy occurred. On a chilly winter evening, Sam and a group of boys were prowling up and down the streets of Hannibal. They came upon a poorly clothed tramp who was obviously drunk from too much whiskey. The raggedy man seemed so pitiful that the boys immediately felt sorry for him.

Thinking that he might make the sad tramp feel better, Sam went away and found some matches. When he returned, he gave them to the tramp so he would be able to light his pipe. Feeling that a good deed had been done, Sam and the other boys went home to go to sleep.

That same night, the tramp was arrested by a Hannibal policeman and put in jail. Lighting a pipe in his drunken state, he set the straw mattress in his jail cell on fire. Before he could be released from the cell, and before the Hannibal Fire Department could put out the blaze, the pitiful tramp burned to death. His horrible screams could be heard throughout much of the town.

Of course, Sam was not directly responsible for the death of the unfortunate man. But for months afterward his sleep was interrupted by nightmares. In the horrible dreams, Sam saw the raggedy man in flames and heard his awful screams of pain and terror.

When he wrote his *Autobiography* more than half a century later, Sam was still trying to make himself feel better about the bitter memory. "The tramp—who was to blame—suffered ten minutes; I who was not to blame, suffered three months." For the millions of people who read Sam's books in later years, it was obvious that he suffered much longer.

By his eighteenth year, Sam's life already seemed like a parade of highs and lows. When things turned out tragically he would think of the long sermons he had heard in church and try to repent. When things went well he would gloat. But one thing was certain. No matter how hard he worked for Orion's newspaper, neither he nor his older brother managed to make much money. Despite the years of hard work, all he had to show for his efforts were empty pockets and shabby clothes.

For some time, Sam had been thinking about leaving Hannibal and looking for better-paying work in a larger city, possibly St. Louis or perhaps even New York. For more than a decade he had watched the glamorous steamboats heading down the Mississippi River for St. Louis and New Orleans. He had seen so many travelers sail down the

Father of Waters. Now, he felt, his time had come.

One day in May of 1853 Jane Clemens held back her tears as she helped her beloved and rambunctious son pack his few belongings before setting sail for the great world beyond Hannibal. The packing completed in a matter of minutes, Jane fetched the family Bible and put Sam's hand on top of it. The mother made her son give a solemn promise that, until his return to Hannibal, he would neither gamble nor drink hard liquor.

Sam would never again live in Hannibal for any length of time. But until his next visit, no one would claim that he had broken that oath made so solemnly to his mother. After that he felt that the promise had been fulfilled and considered himself free to do as he pleased.

Of the world's great writers, probably none wrote as much about his youth as did Sam Clemens. In his later years, when he was known throughout much of the world as Mark Twain, he continued writing about his adventure-filled days in a town along the banks of the mighty Mississippi.

Chapter 3

STEAMBOAT'S A-COMIN'

On a summer morning in 1853 the scene at the Hannibal wharf was the same as it always was before the steamships arrived. Loose dogs and a couple of hogs sniffed around the garbage that lay near the side of the road. Here and there cargo was piled up neatly in preparation for being carried aboard the steamer. Several horse-pulled carriages also awaited the ship and the passengers expected to come ashore from the southbound steamer. Everything was quiet. Store owners lazily rocked back in their chairs waiting for the morning's excitement to begin.

The wide, mighty Mississippi River stretched out endlessly beyond the dock. A mile across the river, the green forests of southern Illinois followed the river's steep banks. At the Missouri dock, eyes strained up and down stream for a glimpse of the steamer. At last came the expected sign. Puffs of dark smoke began to appear above the northern bend in the river. Immediately, a black slave famous all over Hannibal for his keen eye and clear voice shouted the famous call, "Steamboat's a-comin'."

Now the lazy town sprang to life. Children rushed to the wharf to watch the biggest event of the day. Farmers and store owners prepared to meet the ship and place cargo on it or find their deliveries from the north. A number of passengers prepared for boarding.

Sam Clemens lifted his bag and walked toward the wharf as the paddle wheeled ship steamed into view. The long, freshly-painted steamer had two fancy-topped smokestacks that spewed thick smoke over the top deck. Below, young men who watched the boilers opened wide the furnace doors, revealing the fiery red interiors where thick logs burned brightly. The upper deck swarmed with passengers waiting to watch the great ship dock. The captain stood impressively by his huge bell—he was the envy of every boy in Hannibal.

As the steamer approached the dock, the huge paddle wheels stopped turning. When it had almost arrived, the paddle wheels began spinning backwards, churning the river into a bright white foam. The big ship had landed.

Sam quickly followed the other passengers who walked along the wharf and stepped onto the lower deck of the steamboat. In ten minutes, the ship would be steaming down the river once again, and the excitement in Hannibal would be over until the next ship arrived.

But for Sam the adventure of his first journey far from home was just beginning. He had told his mother that he was going to St. Louis, and he was indeed going there. But he knew that his stay would be a brief one. His sights were set much farther to the east. To earn money to continue his voyage, he worked for a short time for the *St. Louis Evening News* in the large office where the newsprint and drawings were typeset and pasted up.

Then it was on to New York, where he arrived with a few dollars of pocket change and a ten dollar bill sewn into the lining of his coat. He had wanted for some time to get to New York to see the World's Fair with its famed Crystal Palace that all the nation was talking about. But the work he found in the big city was less than satisfactory. The small wages he earned at the firm of John A. Gray & Green were barely enough to pay for his room and meals.

Before long, he traveled on to Philadelphia and worked for two different newspapers there. Sam might have had a longer career in the East, but he soon found that Orion desperately needed his help.

Shortly after Sam left Hannibal, his brother Orion had also left the Missouri town. Without Sam to help write and put together the *Journal*, Orion found it almost impossible to produce the little paper. Unable to repay his loan, Orion sold the paper to the old farmer he had borrowed money from. With Henry and his mother, he moved to Muscatine, Iowa. There, he bought an interest in another paper and settled down to a life of grinding poverty.

It was in this situation that Orion practically begged Sam to come and work for him. After only about a year on the East Coast, Sam made a quick sight-seeing trip to Washington, D.C., and then took a train back to St. Louis. Then it was a relatively short trip to the Mississippi River town of Muscatine. Sam helped Orion get settled for a few weeks and then went back to St. Louis to work. In the meantime, the twenty-nine-year-old Orion married a nineteen-year-old girl from Keokuk.

Orion's new wife would hardly settle for life as Orion had always known it. She wanted him to have a better chance at being a business success, and she wanted to live closer to her family. With Jane and Henry, the pair was soon on the move to Keokuk, Iowa, where Orion's wife's family lived. Keokuk was also on the Mississippi River, about fifty miles north of Hannibal. On credit, as always, Orion purchased an interest in a small Keokuk printing shop.

Struggling again, Orion begged Sam to move to Keokuk to help the printing business get better established. For well over a year, Sam worked hard to help his older brother. With Jane at home and young Henry also at work in Orion's office, it must have seemed much like the days in Hannibal.

But Sam still dreamed about seeing the world. He had helped Orion get his business going in Hannibal, in Muscatine, and finally in Keokuk, even though Orion was hardly ever able to pay him the wages he had promised. Sam felt that he should now be free to continue his travels. He read a book about the Amazon River in South America and dreamed about going there. But without the promised wages from Orion, he didn't have the money to buy steamship tickets.

Nevertheless, Sam continued to dream. He eagerly talked to Henry about his plan to explore the Amazon and collect medical plants to sell at a huge profit in America. But it was still a dream until a lucky break came in November of 1856.

On a cold, wintery day Sam was walking down a Keokuk street when his eye was caught by a small slip of paper fluttering in the stiff breeze. To his amazement, he discovered that the paper was a fifty dollar bill. Sam had never seen so much money at one time before.

He put an advertisement in the paper stating that he had found a sum of money and waited anxiously to see if anyone would claim it. When after four days no one did, Sam decided that it was simply a gift to allow him to continue his travels.

He used part of the money to buy a ticket to Cincinnati. There, he worked for about five months to earn a little extra money for his great trip to South America. In April, at the age of twenty-one, Sam used sixteen dollars to buy a ticket on the old steamship *Paul Jones*, which was headed down the Ohio River to the Mississippi and New Orleans. In New Orleans, Sam figured, he would spend the rest of his money to purchase a ticket on the next ship bound for the Amazon River in South America.

The *Paul Jones* was an ancient ship that had seen better

days. For the 1,500-mile voyage to New Orleans, Sam was one of the few passengers aboard. Wiser travelers booked passage on newer ships. Nevertheless, Sam felt that he was now a man of the world, a traveler.

He felt sorry for the young men and women in the Ohio Valley towns he passed along the way. Don't they wish they could be travelers, too, he thought with a smile. When the *Paul Jones* stopped at the landing, Sam leaned casually against the railings on the deck of the old ship. At that spot, he knew the untraveled people in the towns he passed would be sure to see him. When people still didn't watch him, he would sneeze to attract their attention. Then he would stretch and make a mighty yawn to show how bored he was with traveling.

When the *Paul Jones* reached Louisville, Kentucky, it stuck on the rocks in the middle of the river. Sam watched and listened with interest as the crew struggled for four days to free the old tub from the rocky trap. He listened to the officers bark out orders in a strange language familiar only to those who sailed the great rivers. He listened to the crewmen grunt and cuss as they struggled to free the steamer from the rocks.

When the steamer finally pulled into New Orleans, Sam immediately set his sights for South America and the mouth of the Amazon River. Unfortunately, he made two important discoveries. The first was that no one in New Orleans knew of any ship bound for the Amazon within the next ten years. Even more important, he found that the nine or ten dollars remaining in his pocket was not nearly enough for the kind of trip he had been planning.

Sam was crushed. He had been planning to explore the Amazon and earn his fortune there for more than a year. Now he found himself without a career and with little money with which to wait and make a new plan. In a state of near panic, he tried to imagine what he could do.

Then he remembered his boyhood dream back in Hannibal—to be a pilot on a Mississippi riverboat. He remembered how the pilots and captains of the steamers were treated like kings wherever they went. And he knew the wages were higher than for just about any other job in the West. He began to make a plan.

The old *Paul Jones*, the steamer he had traveled on from Cincinnati, was scheduled to sail up the Mississippi River to St. Louis. Sam had already made friends with one of the *Paul Jones*'s pilots, Mr. Bixby. Perhaps he could convince Mr. Bixby to take him on and teach him to be a riverboat pilot.

For three hard days Sam camped out at Mr. Bixby's cabin door, trying his best to show the experienced pilot that he could be an able assistant and a hard worker. Finally, Mr. Bixby gave in. It was agreed that he would teach Sam the river between St. Louis and New Orleans. In exchange, Sam would pay five hundred dollars out of his first earnings as a riverboat pilot for the training.

As the *Paul Jones* backed out of the New Orleans dock at four in the afternoon, Sam was supremely happy. He was beginning one of the great adventures of his life. As soon as he had straightened out the ship and pointed her upstream, Mr. Bixby gave Sam the wheel. He told Sam exactly where to steer the *Paul Jones* to avoid hazards in the dangerous river.

After a while, the steamer passed a bend in the river and Mr. Bixby said, "This is Six-Mile Point." Sam barely listened as they continued steaming up the river. Somewhat later, they passed another bend and Mr. Bixby said, "This is Nine-Mile Point." All these bends and the other things the pilot was pointing out looked pretty much the same to Sam. Not much later, Mr. Bixby said, "This is Twelve-Mile Point" as they passed another bend that looked like all the others. Sam was happy as a clam as he steered the ship according to the pilot's precise instructions.

Pretty soon it was night and a new pilot came to take the wheel. Since steamships traveled all day and all night, pilots took turns at the wheel. When they were off duty, they would return to their cabins and sleep. Sam and Mr. Bixby enjoyed a hearty meal and then crept away to their bunks.

Sam's rest was interrupted at midnight when a lantern was shined in his eyes. "Come! Turn out," the night watchman called. Sam wondered if he could possibly be telling him to get out of bed. He thought that it must be some kind of mistake and went back to sleep. But in just a couple of minutes the watchman returned. This time he fairly shouted his orders for Sam to arise.

Now Sam was really annoyed. "What do you want to come bothering around here in the middle of the night for?" he asked sleepily. "Now as like as not I'll not get to sleep again tonight." But as the watchman left shaking his head, Sam felt that he might be able to get back to sleep. But a few seconds later Mr. Bixby appeared in the cabin. He was raging mad. In an instant Sam was climbing the pilothouse steps still pulling on his clothes. Sam began to fear that piloting might not be quite as much fun as he had imagined.

Guided only by the faint light of the stars, the *Paul Jones* steamed up the wide Mississippi. Sam began to relax a bit. Sleep might be a little difficult, but the work was easy enough. Mr. Bixby seemed to have eyes like a cat, seeing rocks and other dangers in near blackness and showing Sam which way to steer to avoid them.

Suddenly, the pilot whirled around to Sam and asked, "What's the name of the first point above New Orleans?" Sam thought for an instant. He knew that in a test such as this he had to answer directly and without hesitation.

"I don't know, sir," was his firm reply.

"You don't *know*?" Mr Bixby responded, raising his eyebrows. Something in the pilot's tone of voice worried Sam a bit. "Well, you're a smart one," the pilot continued. "What's the name of the next point?"

Now Sam was starting to feel definitely uneasy. He had to admit that he was stumped by that question also. The pilot was turning red with anger.

"Well, this beats anything," Mr. Bixby growled. "Tell me the name of any point or place I told you." When Sam realized that once again he had to admit that he couldn't answer the question, he was beginning to feel awful. But the ordeal was not yet over. The pilot asked several other questions, but Sam could only mumble the same answer as before.

Mr. Bixby was furious. He finally posed his last question to the frightened young man. "What do you know?"

Sam stared at his feet and weakly whispered, "I—I—don't know." With this answer, Mr. Bixby flew into a rage even more terrible than before.

"By the great Caesar's ghost, I believe you!" he screamed. "You're the stupidest dunderhead I ever saw or ever heard of, so help me Moses! The idea of you being a pilot—you! Why, you don't know enough to pilot a cow down a lane."

Sam sincerely hoped that the lesson was over. Mr. Bixby seemed to indicate that it was. He was silently gripping the wheel with tremendous pressure and grinding his teeth in anger. Just when Sam thought that the worst was over, Mr. Bixby whirled toward him again and asked, "Look here!

What do you suppose I told you the names of those points for?"

A number of likely answers occurred to Sam. The one he finally came up with was probably the worst of all the possibilities. "Well—to—to be entertaining, I thought."

With burning ears, Sam was about to discover that the lesson was not yet over. But the description will have to end here. Although Mr. Bixby continued speaking for some time, his language was so precise and colorful that it is hardly appropriate for readers of any age.

By the next day, Sam was holding a notebook and pencil in hand at all times. He made a note of practically everything that Mr. Bixby said. Before long, the book was almost bursting with the names of towns, points, sandbars, islands, bends, and obstacles such as rocks and shipwrecks. But the information was only in the book, not in Sam's head. Even worse, every four hours when he went off duty, there was a four-hour gap in the information the book contained.

When they arrived in St. Louis, Mr. Bixby left the *Paul Jones* and was hired to pilot a larger, much fancier boat. Sam came along with him to the new steamer. Sam had never been in anything quite so elegant. The bright, clean ship had crystal chandeliers and polished brass and wooden fixtures. Eight huge boilers made the steam that powered her shiny engines.

In the magnificent new steamer, Sam, Mr. Bixby, and an

army of crewmembers and passengers headed back down the Mississippi toward New Orleans. Now he was feeling a good deal better about piloting as the ship steamed out of St. Louis. But as Sam returned to the pilothouse wheel, he made another cruel discovery about learning the Mississippi. Here is how he described what he found out.

"When I returned to the pilot-house, St. Louis was gone and I was lost. Here was a piece of river which was all down in my book, but I could make neither head nor tail of it: you understand, it was turned around. I had seen it when coming up-stream, but I had never faced about to see how it looked when it was behind me. My heart broke again, for it was plain that I had got to learn this troublesome river *both ways*."

And learn it he did. Before too many more months, Sam could picture every stretch of the mighty Mississippi between St. Louis and New Orleans with his eyes closed. He knew how the river looked in daylight and at night. Even in the thickest fog, he knew just where the banks and the dangerous shallows were located.

By the time he was entering his second year of training, he knew how the river changed in high water and in low, and how to watch out for ice in the cold months. Most important, he learned from Mr. Bixby how to trust his instincts, to listen to no one other than himself, and to remain calm in even the most dangerous situation.

There was, however, a certain time when all Mississippi pilots had to listen to the voices of others. When the ships were about to enter dangerously shallow waters, a small crew was sent out in a rowboat ahead of the steamer. Following the course the larger ship would soon be taking, the men in the rowboat would drop heavy ropes into the water. Using these ropes, or twains, the men would measure the depth of the water and shout their measurements back to the pilot.

"Mark three!" they would call, indicating fairly deep water. "Quarter less three . . . half twain!" As the water got more and more shallow, the men in the rowboat would call louder to warn of the coming danger. "Quarter twain! Quarter twain! Mark twain!"

The phrase *mark twain* indicated a depth of two fathoms, or twelve feet. That was the depth still considered safe for even a large riverboat. Every captain, pilot, and crewmember on the Mississippi knew exactly what it meant. Soon enough, all the world would call Sam Clemens by his famous pen name, Mark Twain.

It took a world of care to keep a steamboat in safe passage for any length of time. The dangers along the Mississippi were many. Most steamboats, even the grandest, did not last long. Some were cut to pieces by sharp rocks hidden just below the surface of the muddy water. Others crashed into the steep banks during storms or heavy fogs. Many were destroyed when the boilers powering their engines exploded.

Sam was quickly learning that the lives of as many as five hundred people depended on the skill and courage of a steamboat's pilot.

For month after month Sam steered a number of different steamers on the long journey between St. Louis and New Orleans. He learned every peculiarity of the ever-changing river. Each time the ship stopped in St. Louis, Sam visited his mother and Henry, who now were staying with his sister Pamela and her wealthy husband.

Henry was now about twenty and in need of work that would pay a respectable wage. The years he had spent working for Orion had left him, like Sam, with hardly a penny to his name. Feeling that he had found a good line of work on the Mississippi, Sam helped Henry get a job on a riverboat. Henry became a "mud clerk," a position that paid no wages beyond room and board on the steamer. After the training period, however, a mud clerk could move up to a job that paid a good wage.

Sam and Henry occasionally crossed paths on the great river. In the summer of 1858, the two brothers spent a couple of days together guarding the freight docks in New Orleans. A few days later, Henry left aboard the *Pennsylvania*, a steamer headed for St. Louis. Sam left two days later aboard the *A.T. Lacey*. Four days later, one of the greatest tragedies in Sam's life occurred. Just south of Memphis, Tennessee, the ship with Henry aboard exploded in the water. Four of the ship's eight boilers blew up early in the morning, when Henry was asleep. Many of the *Pennsylvania*'s passengers were killed instantly. The terrific explosion sent the front part of the ship high into the air. Henry was badly burned and blown into the river.

When the *A.T. Lacey* arrived in Greenville, Mississippi, Sam learned the awful news. At every stop up the river, Sam desperately sought word of any survivors aboard the *Pennsylvania*. At last he heard that Henry had survived, although badly injured, and was at a makeshift hospital in Memphis. Sam rushed to his brother's bedside.

At first, the doctor thought that Henry would die almost immediately. His skin and lungs had been severely burned by hot steam from the exploding boilers on the ship. Amazingly, Henry clung to life for six days and nights. There was now a slight hope that he would live. On the sixth night after the disaster, the doctor told his medical assistants to give Henry a small dose of morphine, a painkiller, if he had trouble sleeping. The inexperienced medical students gave him an overdose of the dangerous drug. By morning, he was dead.

Sam's heart nearly broke when he discovered that his beloved Henry had died. He thought of the happy days in Hannibal, when he and Henry had played rough and tumble games for hours. He thought of their boisterous contests.

Still feeling the pain months later, Sam received his full pilot's license on September 9, 1858, just before his twenty-third birthday. The agony of his brother's death left little joy for the fact that Sam had become one of the best paid people in the American West.

Earning the remarkable wage of $250 a month, Sam was now a prince of the Mississippi, treated like royalty wherever he went. At every dock, young and old alike would rush to be near him, to hear his stories about the mighty river and to share in his adventures. Despite all the heartaches in his life, his childhood dream to become a pilot on an elegant steamer on the Father of Waters had come true.

Of all the great pilots on the Mississippi, none was more famous or more highly respected than Captain Isiah Sellers. Since the year 1811, when the first steamer had sailed the Mississippi, Captain Sellers had piloted boats on the Big Muddy. Now, the younger men on the river thought that Captain Sellers was like a god.

Isiah Sellers wrote articles for a newspaper called the *New Orleans Picayune*. The stories told about the sights he saw steaming up and down the river. Thinking of the shouts of the men who tested the depth of the river with knotted lengths of rope, Captain Sellers signed his stories, Mark Twain.

Sam read the pieces in the newspaper. Soon his mischievous ways came to the surface once again. He wrote a story poking fun at the way Captain Sellers wrote. He signed it, of course, Mark Twain. Up and down the Mississippi, rivermen read Sam's funny story and laughed at old Captain Sellers. Finally, Isiah himself found a copy of Sam's joke. Hurt by the story, which obviously made fun of him, Captain Sellers would never write another word. Although he had meant no real harm, Sam knew another one of his pranks had caused great sadness.

Sam enjoyed the glorious life of a riverboat pilot for about three years. Although his hair had turned gray shortly after Henry's death, he was still a young man in his middle twenties. He sailed up and down the river, wore fancy silk clothes, told exciting stories about his adventures, and visited sweethearts along his route.

But the times were changing rapidly. In the U.S. Congress, a fierce argument about slavery was brewing. Many politicians in the North wanted to make slavery against the law. Many politicians from the South wanted to keep it legal.

Abraham Lincoln was elected president of the United States in November of 1860. Fearing his antislavery views, the state of South Carolina declared it was no longer a part of the United States just one month later. Within about six months, ten other states from the South followed South Carolina's lead. Lincoln immediately began organizing a huge army in the North. Throughout much of the South, armies were likewise being put together.

Sam took his final voyage on the Mississippi aboard the

steamer *Uncle Sam*. On the vast journey between New Orleans and St. Louis he saw the nation getting ready for war. At Memphis, armed soldiers tried to stop the ship, but somehow it got through. At Vicksburg, Mississippi, Sam had been shocked to find frightened citizens hiding in caves along the river. When it reached St. Louis, the *Uncle Sam* was fired upon and searched by soldiers. The Civil War had begun. It was to be the bloodiest and most bitter war ever fought on American soil.

Although it had not concerned him much when he was young, Sam now had little respect for slavery. Orion had told him for years that it was immoral. And, although Missouri did allow people to own slaves, the state itself voted not to leave the Union.

Sam had heard that the North's Union army was searching for riverboat pilots to be drafted into the war effort. Having little interest in joining an army on either side, Sam hid out for a time with his mother at Pamela's house in St. Louis.

People throughout the state of Missouri were frightened by the thought of war. As a Southern state determined to stay in the Union, Missouri was likely to be invaded by armies from either side. Thousands of people fled the state in panic.

Without saying a word to his mother, Sam traveled to his old hometown of Hannibal. At a secret meeting near Bear

Creek, he talked with more than a dozen of his childhood friends and tried to decide what to do. Each of the friends was determined, above all else, to protect his homeland from invaders. They banded together to form a strange little army called the Marion Rangers. After officers were elected, only three privates were left. Sam became a lieutenant. The Rangers would become a soon forgotten part of the South's Confederate army.

The soldiers in the Marion Rangers had little taste for war. For a few days, they practiced riding on borrowed mules and horses, and then visited local girls in the evening. Without uniforms and with mostly ancient weapons, they did not form much of an army.

In just a few days some farmers warned them that there was a rumor that the Union army was marching in their direction. The Rangers fled in terror, leaving behind most of their weapons, ammunition, and horses. No sooner had they arrived at their new location when another rumor sent them retreating again. Every few days the Marion Rangers ran away from a Union army that was never really there. The soldiers hid in the woods, in corncribs, and behind old farm buildings.

Although he was in no battles, after two weeks Sam had had his fill of war. He deserted the Rangers and returned to St. Louis. There, he discovered that there was astounding news from Orion!

Sam Clemens as an apprentice printer at age 15. This is the earliest known likeness of Sam Clemens.

Left: Sam's mother, Jane Clemens
Below left: Orion Clemens
Below right: Henry Clemens

Samuel Clemens as a riverboat pilot about 1859-60.

Sam's wife, Olivia Langdon Clemens

Sam and Livy had this house built in Hartford, Connecticut. People were amazed as they watched it being built. For one thing, they thought it had too many windows. Nobody could understand why Sam would want the inside of his house to be as bright as day. Reporters joked about how Sam's plans for the house were changed so trees would not be cut down. But it was probably the glass plant room that people made the most fun of. Attached directly to the living room, living plants sent their fragrances into the Clemens home and crickets chirped in the soil. The world laughed as they moved in, but it was the start of seventeen years of happiness for the Clemens family.

The Clemens family left to right: Clara, Olivia, Jean, Sam, and Susy

Mark Twain in 1895

Mark Twain at his old home in Hannibal, Missouri in 1902.

Chapter 4

THE WILD WESTERNER

Jane and Pamela told Sam the exciting news from Orion. An old friend of Orion's named Edward Bates was now a member of President Lincoln's cabinet. Bates used his influence to have Orion named secretary of the territory of Nevada. The office was second only to the governor.

Until just a few years earlier, Nevada had been part of Utah. When rich silver mines were discovered there, many people flocked to the huge county in Utah that is now the state of Nevada. Before long, the new prospectors began squabbling with the Utah government. The tough miners soon tired of the battles and decided to set up their own government separate from Utah.

Faced with the fast developing horror of the Civil War, President Lincoln was anxious to keep as much territory as possible within the Union. With his urging, Congress quickly passed a bill to organize the new Nevada Territory. It was the first step toward becoming a new state in the United States. James W. Nye was named governor of the territory of Nevada. Orion would be his chief assistant and earn the whopping salary of $1,800 a year, not that much less than the wages of a riverboat pilot.

Orion was ready to leave for Nevada but, of course, he had no money for the trip. Knowing that Sam still had savings from his days as a riverboat pilot, Orion offered him a job as his assistant. He quickly accepted and offered his savings to pay for the long trip to Nevada.

In August of 1861, the two brothers began their journey. It started with a steamboat trip up the Missouri River from St. Louis to St. Joseph, Missouri. From there, the fastest transportation west was on the overland stagecoach. The price for a single ticket to Carson City, Nevada, was an astounding $150. Sam paid the fares for himself and Orion.

Even for all that money, passengers were allowed to bring only twenty-five pounds of luggage. The brothers wore as many clothes as they could but still had to ship most of their belongings back to St. Louis. Much of the weight Orion was allowed was taken up by a huge dictionary. He was certain that it would be needed for his new duties in Nevada. After all, he was the secretary of the territory of Nevada.

Sam and the new secretary began their long trip with just one other passenger, a man named George Bemis. Knowing that they would soon be entering hostile Indian country, all three men carried handguns. The stagecoach carried mountains of mail packed in bags piled all over the seats.

In those days, just a few years before the railroad was built across the nation, the overland stage was considered to be a marvel of speed and comfort. All the way to California, coach stations were built just ten miles apart. Every ten miles, a stage hand held a fresh team of six horses at the ready as the stagecoach raced into the next station.

Before long, the stage carrying Sam and the secretary of Nevada crossed the Big Sandy and Little Sandy rivers and raced on into Nebraska, about forty miles from St. Joseph. Even at night and in storms, the coach kept moving through the country. As the trail got rougher, the three passengers were thrown from side to side.

Occasionally, one was struck by the secretary's massive dictionary. The passengers yelled their complaints, but there was no stopping or slowing down. The stagecoach was expected to travel from Missouri to Sacramento, California, a distance of nearly two thousand miles, in little more than two weeks. Occasional cries of pain from inside the coach would seldom stop the impatient driver. The driver, and the conductor who sat next to him at the front of the stage, had to travel many miles without rest before a new driver and conductor would replace them.

Early on the morning of their sixth day out, when they were about 550 miles from St. Joseph, the stagecoach broke down. There would be a delay of five or six hours while repairs were made. The stage hands apologized and offered the passengers some horses to go on a buffalo hunt. But what Sam thought would be an interesting adventure ended in great embarrassment for one of the passengers.

A huge buffalo got angry at George Bemis and began charging him while he was still mounted on his borrowed horse. Not a good shot, Mr. Bemis was chased for about two miles until he finally found a lone tree and climbed it to safety. When he returned to the stage hours later without his horse and lariat, the stage hands roared with laughter. He claimed that the buffalo had climbed the tree after him and that he had been lucky to escape with his life. Sam and Orion laughed, doubting the accuracy of his story.

Soon after the stagecoach started again, the passengers were treated to a view of a pony express rider. In the Old West, nothing moved faster for great distances than the pony express. Following the same route as the stagecoaches, express riders traveled 250 miles at full gallop in a single day. Like the stagecoaches, pony express riders changed to fresh horses every 10 miles, and drivers were changed every 50 miles or so.

The only purpose of the pony express was to carry mail, which had to be written on especially thin paper. A single letter carried the full two-thousand-mile route from Missouri to California needed five dollars in postage. Sam waved frantically to the rider galloping past his stage, but the rider was in too much of a hurry to wave back.

In another day, the stagecoach was in Indian country. The passengers tightly shut the blinds inside the coach and talked nervously. That night, their nervous sleep was broken by a gunshot. Then there was a horrible scream.

"Help! Help! Help!" yelled their driver, several yards to the side of the coach.

"Kill him! Kill him like a dog!" a gruff voice yelled.

"I'm being murdered!" the driver screamed in terror. "Will no man lend me a pistol?"

There were more gunshots. The passengers inside the coach shivered with fright. Suddenly, a whip cracked loudly near the front of the stage and it began to move again. Soon it was thundering through the night. The passengers screamed, begging the conductor to tell them what had happened. He refused.

The next morning, the conductor explained. When the passengers were awakened by gunshots, the stage had been at a station where a new driver was coming aboard. The old driver got off without his pistol and was soon attacked by bandits awaiting his arrival at the station. In such cases, the drivers had instructions to take off immediately, no matter what.

It was a chilling story. No one knew for certain what happened to the old driver, but everyone feared the worst. Now the passengers and stage hands began talking about bandits that roamed the lawless West. As he heard the awful stories about gunslingers and desperadoes, Sam lost all interest in worrying about Indians. Each gunslinger the stage hands named sounded more terrible than the last. The most fearsome of all, they finally agreed, was a man simply called "Slade." Just the sound of the name made Sam shiver. Slade!

Here was a gunslinger, the stage hands said, who had killed twenty-six men, many of them shot in the back. Sometimes a man would say just a single wrong word to Slade, and in an instant that man would be dead. Slade was so feared throughout the West that the stagecoach company had hired him to protect the company's property along a particularly lawless stretch of the route.

After a while, the bloody conversation about gunslingers faded away and the passengers settled down among the sacks of mail to sleep. In the morning, the stage pulled into a station where breakfast would be served. Sam, Mr. Bemis, and the new secretary of Nevada walked into the tiny shack ready for a hearty meal.

Inside, they found a half dozen rough-looking men, bearded mountaineers from the Rockies and a few stage hands. All looked as if they had lived in the wilds for years. All except one, that is.

One man in the small crowd was well dressed and clean shaven. He seemed to be the person in charge and everyone tried to please him. One of the station hands looked at the clean shaven man and said, "Coffee's ready, Mr. Slade."

Slade! The name pierced Sam's heart like an arrow. Here he was sitting down to breakfast with a man who had killed twenty-six men! Sam lost all taste for his food, but he ate anyway. He certainly didn't want to offend anyone, particularly Slade.

Sam ate his food and drank his coffee in silence, although Slade asked politely if all the passengers were enjoying the trip. Slade was about to pour himself the last of the coffee from the pot when he noted that Sam's cup was empty. He offered to fill it.

Sam was close to panic. If he said no, Slade might get angry. If he said yes, soon enough Slade might decide that he wanted the coffee for himself. Either way Sam imagined that he would soon be number twenty-seven on Slade's list of dead men. Fortunately, Slade insisted that Sam take the coffee. Sam finished his breakfast without further incident. When they were ready to go, Slade came out to the stage to wish the travelers a good journey. Sam never saw him again, but he heard a few years later that Slade had been hanged, and had cried like a baby just before he died.

Before long the stagecoach was high in the Rocky Mountains. For the first time, Sam saw one of his boyhood dreams: snow covering the rocky peaks in the middle of the summer. He was astonished to see human skeletons all along the route. The skeletons were the last remains of pioneers who had died trying to cross the mountains. At night, the phosphorus in the old bones made them glow like Halloween masks. The sight made all the passengers shudder.

Soon the stage was rushing down the western slopes of the mountains. Beyond was the desert and, eventually, Salt Lake City in Utah. Sam and the secretary suffered from the awful desert heat. All along the trail were human skeletons bleached pure white by the blazing sun. They were the bones of the pioneers who hadn't made it to California and the bones of miners who, in 1849 and 1850, had died trying to reach the gold and silver mines of the fabled West.

Finally, at around noon on the twentieth day of their trip, the stagecoach pulled into Carson City, the new home of the new secretary of Nevada. Sam was sad that the exciting trip had ended. He wasn't too impressed by the looks of his new hometown. Carson City was in the middle of the desert, surrounded by mountains. There wasn't a tree anywhere in sight, yet the entire town, even the sidewalks, was made of wood.

In the days that followed, Sam explored the countryside while Orion settled down to his work as secretary of Nevada. Some of the men in the boardinghouse where Sam stayed told him about a magnificent lake nearby, called Lake Tahoe. Sam explored the land around the crystal clear lake and marveled at its beauty.

The law of the territory said that a man could claim land for his own if he built a fence around it and put up a house in the middle. Sam and a friend cut down some trees near Lake Tahoe. Where the trees fell was their "fence." Then the friends made a little house out of shrubs and bushes, a project that took only a few hours. Perhaps, Sam thought, it would be enough to satisfy the law so that he could call this beautiful land his own. Unfortunately, a few days later a campfire went out of control and burned down all the "improvements" Sam and his friend had made.

Back in Carson City, Orion wasn't having much better luck. One of the new secretary's first duties was to rent a building where the Territorial Congress could meet. But no one who owned a suitable building had much trust in the federal government. No one seemed to believe that the bills for rent would be paid. Just when it appeared that the new congress would have to meet in the middle of the desert, a wealthy patriot offered a building free. But the secretary had to use his own money to buy a canvas curtain to separate the House of Representatives from the Senate. When the secretary hired an Indian to cut firewood for the new legislature, the U.S. government refused to pay the bill! Once again, Orion had to pay out of his own pocket.

It was examples such as this, and many others, that caused Sam to lose his interest in the new government of the territory of Nevada. But there was something of great interest to him in the area.

For years, prospectors around Nevada had been striking it rich by finding silver in the hills around Carson City. Sam listened intently to prospectors' stories about fabulous discoveries. Men dressed in rags one day claimed to be worth millions the next. Everyone in Carson City was talking about vast lodes of silver recently discovered in the Esmerelda mines. Sam was thinking about going to the Esmerelda mines when a new story broke about an even more fabulous mine in Humboldt County, about two hundred miles northeast of Carson City.

A local newspaper, the *Daily Territorial Enterprise*, reported that a ton of diggings from the Humboldt mines had earned as much as seven thousand dollars in silver for the lucky prospectors. Sam could no longer stand idly by just listening to the stories. Borrowing some money form Orion, he and three partners struck out for Humboldt County in December of 1861.

Winter in the Nevada hills was cold and snowy. In the bitter weather, Sam and his partners claimed a mine and dug for weeks. They found no silver, but Sam discovered worthless "fool's gold" a number of times. Soon they tired of the work and traveled to other mines in the area. But when no rich silver strikes were made, Sam and his partners decided to give up. They would return to Carson City and travel to the more promising Esmerelda mines, a trip of several hundred miles.

Soon after they began the long trip to Carson City, a blinding snowstorm struck. Almost immediately, the men were lost. On horseback, they rode and rode, able to see only a few feet in front of them. When they just about had lost all hope, they found a set of fresh hoofprints in the thick blanket of snow. They cheered at the sight! They could follow the prints all the way to Carson City.

Greatly relieved, the men rode at a near gallop, anxious for a warm fire and a hearty meal. Before long, the tracks they were following became more numerous. Other riders must have joined the group traveling ahead of them. Sam and his partners rushed on into the blinding snowstorm. Soon, there were even more tracks, some amazingly fresh. At that point, one of the riders began to worry. He got down off his horse and studied the tracks carefully. Then he made an awful discovery. The tracks were their own. The partners had been traveling in circles, following the hoofprints of their own horses! They were no closer to Carson City than they had been hours and hours earlier.

The exhausted prospectors were forced to make a camp in the snow-covered desert. Without a chance of lighting a fire, each man knew that he was in danger of freezing to death. The men tried desperately to stay awake, knowing all too well that sleep could drift into death without warning. Sam tried as best he could to stay awake, but finally he could not fight his sleepiness any longer.

In a few hours, all the men awoke. One of the partners was hollering and screaming. The others looked where he was pointing frantically. There, the faint dawn light showed a stagecoach station, just a few yards away from them. They had spent the terrible night just steps away from a warm room!

Sam and his partners returned safely to Carson City. But before long, Sam was off again to strike it rich. This time he headed for the famous Esmerelda mines. But once again, although he saw others discover silver mines worth fortunes, he had no luck himself. During the year of 1862, he spent most of his time searching for the precious metal. His greatest success was not found with a pickax and shovel but was, as always, produced from pen and paper. For some months, he had been sending humorous letters to the *Daily Territorial Enterprise*, the most popular newspaper in Nevada. The editors at the newspaper liked the exaggerated style of the letters and printed many of them.

Before long, the owner of the newspaper offered Sam a job as a reporter. The salary, twenty-five dollars a week, was higher than anything Sam had earned in more than a year of prospecting. He happily accepted the job and walked to Virginia City, where the newspaper's offices were located.

Virginia City, Nevada, was fast becoming one of the great boom towns of the West. One of the richest veins of silver in the nation, called the Comstock Lode, was buried directly beneath the town. Miles of tunnels were dug under nearly every street and building.

Sam worked for the *Enterprise* by writing two columns for each edition of the paper. As he had done everywhere else, he "improved" the news to make it funny and interesting. Many of his stories were totally untrue. In them, he would make fun of popular beliefs and exaggerate his "facts" to such an extent that it seems impossible that anyone would actually believe they were true. Surprisingly, almost everyone believed nearly everything he wrote.

In one story, for example, Sam made fun of petrified fossils. Petrified fossils, in case you didn't know, are the remains of plants or animals that were once alive. When buried underground, the remains gradually were petrified, or turned to stone. Many people around Virginia City were interested in finding little pieces of petrified fossils.

Sam thought the little chunks of petrified rock were interesting, too. But, he thought, they weren't quite interesting enough for one of his stories. So he set out to "improve" them. Sam wrote a story about a petrified prospector who had been found, full size, thumbing his nose at the town. He didn't think anyone would believe such a wild tale, which he wrote, of course, as a joke. But nearly everyone did believe it. Sam's story of the petrified prospector was copied in newspapers throughout the West. It even appeared in a paper in London, England. The world was astounded! Sam must have been pretty surprised himself.

The name of Sam Clemens was already becoming pretty

well known in the West when he heard a piece of sad news from the Virginia City telegraph office. Old Captain Isiah Sellers, the famous Mississippi riverboat pilot, had died. Sam remembered the proud old man who had signed his newspaper articles as "Mark Twain." And he remembered how hurt the captain had been when he read Sam's story making fun of him in a New Orleans newspaper. Sam decided to honor the old captain by signing many of his stories "Mark Twain." From that time on, Mark Twain became Sam's pen name. Nearly everything he wrote was signed with that old riverboat call.

Sam was pleased to be working for a newspaper in the territory of Nevada. From back east in "the States," news came of the terrible bloodshed and fighting of the Civil War. More than half a million people were killed in that cruel war, and Sam might well have been one of them had he not come to the West.

In Nevada, his Mark Twain pen name was becoming famous. Politicians and wealthy prospectors were anxious to be mentioned in his popular columns. His salary was soon raised to forty dollars a week, higher than that paid to the secretary of Nevada. But as it had so many times in the past, Sam's mischievous sense of humor landed him in trouble.

In April of 1864, the editor of his newspaper decided to visit San Francisco. Sam was left in charge of the *Enter-*

prise. The trouble started out innocently enough. Looking for topics to write an editorial on, Sam discovered that the very next morning was the three hundredth anniversary of the birth of William Shakespeare. Although few people in Nevada knew who Shakespeare was, Sam decided to change all that. In his *Autobiography*, Sam described what happened next.

"I got the Cyclopaedia and examined it and found out who Shakespeare was and what he had done, and I borrowed all that .... There wasn't enough of what Shakespeare had done to make an editorial of the necessary length but I filled it out with what he hadn't done—which in many respects was more important and striking and readable than the handsomest things he had really accomplished."

Despite all the hard work Sam put into his article about Shakespeare, the very next morning found him in need of yet another editorial. Afraid that he was running out of ideas to write about, he had a sudden inspiration. He would insult the owner of the rival newspaper, The *Union* of Virginia City. In his editorial, Sam proved that he was a master at the art of insulting people. The next day, the owner of The *Union*, a Mr. Laird, returned the insults in his own editorial.

When they read Mr. Laird's editorial, the young men working in Sam's office got very excited. In the American West of the time, many arguments were settled with a duel, a way of fighting in which two grown men stood a few steps apart and fired guns at each other. For many of the uneducated people in Nevada, shooting a man was considered about the bravest and best thing anyone could do.

All day long, Sam's assistants waited for Mr. Laird to challenge Sam to a duel. As the hours went by and no challenge came, they became sadder and sadder. Perhaps there wouldn't be a duel after all. The younger workers were surprised to see Sam's spirits rise as it became less likely that there would be a duel. They figured Sam must be one of the strongest men in the world to hide his feelings so.

Finally, Sam's assistants decided to act. Without checking first with Sam, they offered Mr. Laird a challenge. Laird was an expert shot and thought the duel would be unfair. He accepted the challenge only after much arguing. A duel was scheduled for 5:00 the next morning.

Fortunately for Sam, who was a terrible shot, the duel never occurred. Sam's friends at the newspaper managed to trick Mr. Laird into thinking that Sam was a supermarksman. Mr. Laird quickly backed down and went back to work. Sam did the same.

But Sam's troubles were just beginning. Nevada politicians, anxious to seem more civilized so that their territory could become a state, had just passed a law against dueling. A friend of the Nevada governor sent word to Sam that he would be put in jail for two years if he did not get on the next stagecoach out of town.

The overland stagecoach left for San Francisco at 4:00 the next morning. Sam had more than one reason to be on it. In the brief period during which he had been in charge of editorials for the *Enterprise*, Sam had managed to outrage six men. One, besides Mr. Laird, threatened to kill him. The others wanted to beat him up. Sam left Virginia City before dawn, realizing that he had overstayed his visit in Nevada. Even at that early hour, a crowd of friends gathered at the stagecoach station to wish Sam good-bye.

Sam got a job with a San Francisco newspaper, but he was soon fired. Now nearly thirty, Sam was once again in trouble. Without a job and with little money saved, Sam was uncertain about his future. Orion was, as usual, unable to help. When Nevada became a state in 1864, Orion could certainly have become secretary of state. But Sam's older brother thought that campaigning was undignified, and he did nothing to advance his cause. He didn't get one single vote. Now he was trying to support himself and his family, who had also moved out to Nevada, from his meager law practice. Orion was so honest that nobody wanted to hire him.

In desperation, Sam returned to prospecting. But instead of looking for silver this time, he searched for gold in the California hills. The results in California were as disappointing as they had been in Nevada. A few others became rich, but Sam found only hunger and poverty.

Although there was little money, prospecting offered good conversation and fun with some of the other miners. In one mining camp, Sam heard a silly story. It was about a man who had a frog that he entered into jumping contests and about the time someone poured buckshot into the frog so it couldn't jump. Sam wrote up the silly story in a piece he called "The Celebrated Jumping Frog of Calaveras County." The story created a sensation. It was printed in newspapers throughout the West. In two years, it would become the lead story in Sam's first book.

Sam must have enjoyed writing the story. By the spring of 1865, at the age of thirty, he finally knew what he wanted to do. He planned to see the world—and to write stories that would make the world laugh.

Chapter 5

THE WORLD TRAVELER

Sam returned to San Francisco with a purpose. He would see the world and make his name by writing humorous stories. But first, he had to pay off debts that had developed from his worthless year as a prospector.

In San Francisco, Sam was hired by the *Daily Territorial Enterprise*, the newspaper he had worked for in Virginia City, Nevada. He wrote humorous letters to the paper describing his life in San Francisco. The paper was well pleased by Sam's stories, and soon his debts were paid. Now his new adventures could begin in earnest.

Sam's next job, and his next adventure, was one that many people would envy today. He made a deal with the *Sacramento Union* newspaper to send him to the Sandwich Islands, now called Hawaii. Once a week, Sam was to write a letter to the paper telling about the sights he saw during the trip. He would be paid twenty dollars per letter.

As Mark Twain, Sam traveled with thirty other passengers aboard the propeller-driven steamship *Ajax*, crossing two thousand miles of the Pacific. In March of 1866, all the passengers aboard the *Ajax* swarmed to the upper deck to see the first glimpse of Diamond Head, an old volcano on the island of Oahu. They had arrived at the tropical paradise called, then, the Sandwich Islands.

For nearly half a year, Sam explored the Sandwich Islands. On horseback, he was surprised to find how small the famous islands were. Riding six or eight miles in any direction always brought him to the blue Pacific Ocean and the sandy beaches that surrounded each island.

Exploring the islands of Hawaii, Oahu, and Maui, Sam saw the big sugar, fruit, and coffee farms where small fortunes could be made by sending goods back to California. He marveled at the palm trees, thick jungles, exotic plants, and beautiful tropical flowers. He saw Mauna Loa, the largest active volcano in the world. He was fascinated by volcanoes, the tall, cone-shaped mountains that belched smoke and fire from deep beneath the earth's surface.

Sam climbed to the top of a volcano called Kilauea and looked down into the fiery crater at its center. There he saw molten lava, rock so hot that it glows red and flows like thick gravy in a huge bowl. Although his native guides refused to stay, Sam and a friend walked down into the crater of Kilauea. The surface was hot, and bright red lava and plumes of dark smoke and steam were all around. Sam and his friend spent an entire night camping in the unearthly crater. Sam was so impressed by the Sandwich Islands' mighty volcanoes that he climbed yet another one, called Haleakala. When he reached the top, he saw the world's largest crater, nearly thirty miles across.

The *Sacramento Union* newspaper was delighted with Sam's interesting and often funny stories. They paid him a good deal more than they had promised. In the Sandwich Islands, Sam had to pay all his own expenses. When he arrived back in San Francisco in August of 1866 he was, once again, nearly broke. Word from Orion back in Nevada was no better.

Sam had little money, but his fame along the West Coast was spreading. His "Jumping Frog" story had created a sensation as it was copied in newspaper after newspaper. The pieces about the Sandwich Islands he had written under the name of Mark Twain had been read throughout California and Nevada. Because he was so well known, a man who owned theaters in California suggested that Sam could earn money by giving lectures about his trip. Sam thought about the idea and decided it was worth a try. He had an advertisement printed for his first lecture. The ad ended with this remark: "Admission one dollar; doors open at half past seven, the trouble begins at eight."

The trouble began before eight. Sam arrived at the theater two hours early and was extremely nervous. When he finally walked out on stage, he faced a large audience and froze. For several minutes he could say nothing.

Finally he began to speak in his slow, almost peculiar drawl. As he spoke he regained his courage. Soon he was on his way, "improving" his already interesting story at every opportunity. He was relieved when the large crowd roared with laughter at things he had only hoped were funny. For more than an hour, he held the audience in his pocket. Before his speech was over, he began to understand his power as a public speaker. Virtually at will, he could make the crowd ripple with laughter, or gasp with fright, or simply smile.

Sam's lecture was very popular with the audience that heard it. Now everyone wanted to hear the well-known writer speak. For several weeks, Sam toured California and Nevada giving his famous talk. He spoke in San Francisco, Sacramento, and in smaller towns with strange names such as Red Dog, You Bet, and Gold Hill. In just a few weeks, he had earned $1,500, nearly an entire year's wages for the secretary of the territory of Nevada. With enough money to continue his travels, Sam's dream to see the world was renewed. He visited the office of the *Daily Alta California* newspaper and made a deal with the owners. The newspaper would publish fifty letters Sam would write during his travels and pay him $20 for each letter.

Sam planned to take a steamship to China but thought that he should visit his mother and Pamela in St. Louis before he left. Pamela's wealthy husband had died at a surprisingly young age. Without his income, the two widows had to struggle to make ends meet.

Rather than take the long, hard overland route to St. Louis, Sam decided to go all the way to New York by ship and then travel back westward to St. Louis. After he landed, Sam met some of the members of New York's famous Plymouth Church. One of the Sunday school teachers at the church was also a steamship captain. His name was Charles C. Duncan. Captain Duncan was organizing a trip to the Holy Land and Europe aboard the steamship *Quaker City*.

The *Quaker City* expedition was being organized so that wealthy leaders of Protestant churches could visit the lands where Jesus had lived and preached. But Sam looked at the trip in a somewhat different light. By joining the voyage, he could see much of the world and write his letters to the *Daily Alta California*. He also knew that the other members of the expedition would themselves be interesting. It would be fun to write about faraway places as well as the Americans who were visiting them.

Sam put down a deposit on the $1,250 fee for a ticket aboard the *Quaker City*. But since the ship would not be sailing for some time, Sam used the opportunity to travel to St. Louis to visit his mother and sister Pamela. It had been six years since he had last seen them, and as gifts he brought a Hawaiian Bible and a necklace.

Even as far east as St. Louis, Sam had already achieved some amount of fame as a writer. His newspaper letters about the Sandwich Islands and his story, "The Celebrated

Jumping Frog of Calaveras County," had been widely read. Partly because of this, Sam was invited to lecture in St. Louis to help raise money for a church. He grabbed the opportunity to improve his skills as a lecturer.

Throughout his life, Sam was never afraid to shock people in order to get their attention. In St. Louis, he announced that at his lecture he would follow a custom he had learned while visiting the Sandwich Islands. He announced that he would *eat* the firstborn child of any mother attending the lecture who was willing to give up her baby. When he finally delivered his talk, Sam tried to act surprised that no mother in the audience was willing to surrender her child. Despite that disappointment, the lecture was a great success.

During his brief visit to the Mississippi Valley, Sam returned for a talk in his old hometown of Hannibal. He was surprised to find that the little city had fallen on hard times. The Civil War had ended riverboat traffic on the river. All over the nation, men were busy building railroads. As yet, none had come to Hannibal. The town suffered from the loss. Sam also made a quick trip to Keokuk, where signs had been put up welcoming home America's greatest humorist.

The *Quaker City* steamship was scheduled to leave New York on June 8, 1867. Sam said his good-byes to Jane and Pamela well ahead of the departure date and returned to New York.

When he arrived, a check for the balance he owed on the

price of the steamship ticket was awaiting him from the *Daily Alta California*. At nearly the same time his first book was published. It was called *The Celebrated Jumping Frog of Calaveras County and Other Sketches*. At first Sam thought it would do extremely well, but he was soon disappointed. Total sales were fewer than four thousand copies.

A short time later, Sam was aboard the *Quaker City* anxious to see the world. During the ten-thousand-mile trip, he would be writing humorous letters to three newspapers, the *Herald* and the *Tribune* of New York and, of course, the *Daily Alta California*.

A crowd of well-wishers were at the docks of New York harbor on Saturday, June 8. They waved good-bye to the religious travelers from New England, New York, and as far west as the Mississippi Valley. Altogether, fifteen different states were represented on board the *Quaker City*. By afternoon, the steamship, its sails neatly folded below the deck, cruised out of New York harbor.

In less than an hour, the ship stopped and dropped its anchor. It was pouring down rain and the waves of the Atlantic Ocean were being whipped up by strong winds.

For the rest of the evening and all during Sunday, the *Quaker City* lay at anchor at the mouth of New York harbor. On Sunday morning, Sam went early to breakfast to catch sight of his fellow passengers. He was surprised to find that most of the travelers were relatively old.

On Monday morning, Captain Duncan ordered the anchor raised. The *Quaker City*'s engines strained as the ship headed out of the harbor and into the open Atlantic.

Although the ship rocked and swayed so severely it was hard to walk on its decks, Sam went outside his cabin to greet some of the other passengers. But as he tried to say "Hello" to the people he met, they merely grabbed their stomachs and reeled away. Later, Sam described his first discovery about his shipmates:

"I knew what was the matter with them. They were seasick. And I was glad of it. We all like to see people seasick when we are not, ourselves. . . . By some happy fortune I was not seasick. That was a thing to be proud of."

As the long voyage continued, Sam began to notice that many of the passengers seemed to be determined to avoid having a good time. Dancing was allowed for the first three evenings, although it was often difficult to stand on the heaving and swaying floor. After that, the passengers voted and decided that dancing was sinful and was therefore banned for the rest of the trip. Prayer meetings and "respectable" card games, not poker, were more than enough to satisfy the need for an evening's entertainment.

In his notes and letters, Sam began to make fun of the stiff and mostly humorless passengers aboard the *Quaker City*. As the ship sailed on and on, Sam grew increasingly irritated with his boring shipmates.

Finally, at 3:00 on the morning of June 21, Sam and the rest of the passengers were awakened from their sleep. The small group of islands called the Azores were in view. The Azores are a group of nine islands in the middle of the Atlantic Ocean, nearly a thousand miles from Europe. Sam and his shipmates explored the islands on donkeys.

By the early morning of June 30, a full week after leaving the tiny Azores, land was once again in sight. Within an hour after the passengers first glimpsed the southern shore of Europe, the *Quaker City* was steaming into the Straits of Gibraltar. Passing through the narrow ribbon of ocean, only thirteen miles wide at its narrowest point, the travelers could see the continent of Europe to their left and the continent of Africa to their right. The *Quaker City* steamed on into the Mediterranean Sea.

When the ship stopped at the towering Rock of Gibraltar, Sam and his shipmates explored the famous mountain of rock. More than seven thousand British soldiers wearing bright red coats were stationed there. The Rock of Gibraltar had been famous throughout much of history because no ships could enter or leave the Mediterranean Sea without passing almost directly below it. Huge cannons aimed at the sea were built into spaces carved out of the rock.

From Gibraltar, Sam traveled to Tangier on the coast of Africa. But the whirlwind tour the *Quaker City* was making required a tight schedule. Before long, the ship was sailing across the narrow Mediterranean toward France. Sam and his shipmates celebrated the Fourth of July aboard ship in the middle of the Mediterranean.

When the *Quaker City* landed at the French port of Marseilles, Sam and some of the others explored the sights and then traveled through France by train, finally arriving at the famous city of Paris. The shipmates lingered for a few precious days in Paris, where they saw Emperor Napoleon III and saw the art treasures in the world's most famous museum, the Louvre.

The excursionists hurried back to the *Quaker City* and sailed on to Italy. In the Italian city of Milan, they came upon an old church in bad repair. Inside, a number of artists had set up easels and were making copies of a huge, faded painting about thirty feet long. The big painting was *The Last Supper* by Leonardo da Vinci. The famous painting was old and faded; the newer copies were bright and colorful. Sam joked that all the younger painters in the church must have been greater than da Vinci, because their paintings looked much better than his.

By rail, the shipmates traveled on to Venice. In the ancient city that had watery canals instead of streets, Sam rode by gondola, a kind of long and pointed boat, to his hotel. But there was little time for dallying anywhere with the tight schedules the travelers had to keep. Soon they were off for Rome.

Sam was enchanted by the Eternal City of Rome. But he couldn't resist making fun of all the things that were supposed to impress tourists who visited them. People would soon be reading his letters on both coasts of the United States and would be laughing as Sam poked fun at the Old Masters, the ruins of famous buildings, the people in far-away lands, his shipmates, and himself. But despite the jokes, Sam was reluctant to leave the beautiful and ancient city of Rome.

Before he left Italy, the old volcano-climber himself couldn't resist visiting Vesuvius, the only active volcano on the European mainland. When he reached the top, Sam peered down into the famous crater. He couldn't help writing that the crater, which everyone made a big deal about in Europe, was more like a ditch. He felt that Vesuvius was a pretty sorry volcano compared with the magnificent ones in the Sandwich Islands. Sam's tour of Italy ended with a visit to Pompeii, an ancient city that had been completely buried when Vesuvius erupted.

As the *Quaker City* steamed across the Ionian Sea toward Greece, Sam continued poking fun at Europe in his letters to the American newspapers. Despite his jokes, Sam was so impressed by France and Italy that he chose to spend considerable time in the two countries late in his life.

Sam saved his meanest jokes for the passengers aboard the *Quaker City*. Once, when the ship was heading into a stiff wind that slowed its progress, Sam saw a group of very religious passengers praying that the wind would stop. Sam wrote about how surprised he was that Christians would make such a prayer. After all, if the wind stopped, then sailing boats going in the opposite direction from the *Quaker City* would not be able to continue. He thought it was highly un-Christian for people aboard a steamship to pray for favorable winds.

When the ship reached the Greek shore, it headed directly for the ancient city of Athens. One of the most famous buildings in the world was there, the more than two-thousand-year-old Parthenon. But when the ship got as close to Athens as possible, a problem arose. Fearing the spread of disease, Greek officials would not allow the *Quaker City* passengers to come ashore.

Sam refused to miss an opportunity to see the Parthenon. At night, he and a few shipmates crept off the boat and walked up the famous hill called the Acropolis. When they were near the top, they managed to get through a guarded fence and walk into the moonlit Parthenon. Sam was overwhelmed by its majesty. For once, no jokes occurred to him. On the way back to the ship, Sam and his friends were followed by Greek farmers carrying guns.

The *Quaker City* continued its voyage east, first stopping at Constantinople (called Istanbul today) and then continuing through the Black Sea to Yalta on the southern coast of

Russia. The shipmates traveled to the summer palace of the Russian czar. There, Sam shook hands personally with Alexander II, emperor of Russia.

When the *Quaker City* steamed out of Yalta, it was at last headed for the Holy Land, the area described so often in the Bible and the books of other great religions. When the goal was reached, Sam and seven of his shipmates started out on horseback to see the Bible country. Even in the Holy Land, Sam continued making fun of the things he saw. He also suffered terribly from the desert heat. In his letters back to California and New York, Sam poked the most fun at his shipmates:

"But of all the ridiculous sights I ever have seen, our party of eight is the most so," he wrote. "They travel single file; they all wear the endless white rag of Constantinople wrapped round and round their hats and dangling down their backs; they all wear thick green spectacles, with side-glasses to them; they all hold white umbrellas, lined with green, over their heads .... I wouldn't let any such caravan go through a country of mine."

On his ten-thousand-mile trip, Sam saw the same sights that most other sightseers saw. But he wrote about them in such an interesting and humorous way that even the few experienced travelers of the time could think about the familiar sights anew after reading Sam's descriptions.

Sam didn't see his most memorable sight until the *Quaker City* had already started the long trip home. What excited him the most wasn't a church, or a castle, or the chance to make fun of his shipmates; it wasn't even a volcano. What excited him most was the picture of a girl.

Sam had become friends with an eighteen-year-old boy named Charlie Langdon who was also traveling on the *Quaker City*. Charlie showed Sam an ivory miniature of his only sister, Olivia. Sam was immediately bewitched by the girl he had never seen in person.

Sam told Charlie that Olivia was the most beautiful girl he had ever seen. He begged Charlie to help him meet her. When Charlie answered that he would try to have Sam invited for dinner around Christmas, a time when the Langdon family usually visited New York City, Sam could barely contain his excitement. Still, he would have to wait three months to meet the beautiful young girl.

The *Quaker City* steamed into New York harbor on November 19, 1867. On the exciting return trip, Sam had stopped off to walk among the pyramids of Egypt. It had been an exciting voyage. But now, most of the passengers were glad to be rid of Sam. Sam was glad to finally have the chance to escape from their boring lives. Sam's final opinion of the cruise was that it had been like a "funeral excursion without a corpse." But Sam had little time now for quarrels with his ex-shipmates.

He had two very important things on his mind. First was to write a long book about his adventures aboard the *Quaker City*. But he was also looking forward to his meeting with Olivia Langdon, Charlie's sister, now only about a month away. He remembered the beautiful ivory miniature of Olivia he had seen while on the *Quaker City*.

But other things were even more pressing. Before he had taken his cruise, Sam was offered a job in Washington, D.C., as a secretary for a U.S. senator. Although he knew the wages would be low and the work would not be very exciting, Sam accepted. Working for the senator, he thought he might be able to find some sort of job for Orion in the capital city of Washington.

Sam traveled to Washington and worked briefly for the senator. But it didn't work out right. With the fame his *Quaker City* letters had brought, Sam could earn far more money than a secretary's wages merely by giving lectures. He quit before Christmas.

Christmastime brought the long-awaited meeting with Olivia Langdon. Sam traveled to the fancy hotel in New York City where Olivia and her wealthy family were spending the holidays. The minute he saw the twenty-two-year-old girl, called "Livy" by her friends and family, Sam fell in love. She was beautiful, delicate, and intelligent.

For her part, Livy wasn't sure what to think of Sam.

Although she told her brother Charlie that there was much to be admired about him, Sam's unusual ways confused her. Livy had been brought up in a strictly religious home. Sam's jokes about the Holy Land seemed wild and unwise to her. There was also a question about Sam's patriotism. He seemed to poke fun at just about everything Livy had learned to honor.

Sam had no misgivings whatsoever about Livy. Although an ice skating accident a few years earlier had left her paralyzed, Livy had learned to walk again with the help of a faith healer after doctors had given up hope. Although her body was frail and weak, Sam loved her inner strength and strong convictions. Sam talked with Livy and her father for some time. Livy's father, Jervis Langdon, liked Sam immediately.

After that first meeting, Sam could wait only a few days before seeing Livy again, this time at a New Year's party also in New York City. He stayed for the entire day and part of the evening, unable to tear himself away from Livy.

With the holidays over, Livy and her family went back to their home in upstate Elmira. Reluctantly, Sam went back to Washington, D.C., to earn money anyway he could and work on his book about the *Quaker City* trip. Sam had decided to call his second book *The New Pilgrim's Progress*, but Livy suggested another title, *The Innocents Abroad*. Using his newspaper letters and notes as material, Sam worked furiously to write the long book, sometimes typing as many as thirty pages in a single night.

Sam had been invited to visit Livy and her family at the Langdon home in Elmira, New York. As soon as he finished correcting his final draft of *The Innocents Abroad*, Sam handed the thick manuscript to the American Publishing Company and rushed to Elmira. Almost as soon as he saw her, he proposed marriage. Livy turned him down.

Sam stayed on at the large Langdon house in Elmira for two weeks, but he could not convince Livy to marry him. Sadly, he said good-bye to her and traveled to St. Louis to visit his mother and widowed sister. When he first arrived, he was very unhappy. But a letter from Livy sent his spirits soaring. Uninvited, he rushed back to Elmira.

Livy's father, Jervis Langdon, had liked Sam since the first time he met him, but he was not pleased to greet the uninvited guest this time. Sam was welcomed to stay only briefly. He proposed to Livy again, and was again turned down. Then Sam got a lucky break that brought back his mischievous ways. As he was leaving the Langdon home, a horse pulling the wagon he was riding in suddenly bolted. Sam was thrown to the ground on his head.

He wasn't injured a bit, but he pretended that he was. He was carried into the Langdon mansion where Livy took care of him for three days. Sam was in heaven, but soon enough the doctors insisted that he was fit to travel.

When he left Elmira, Sam was able to earn good wages by lecturing. Whatever time he had between talks must have been spent writing to Livy. In all, he wrote nearly two hundred letters to her during his courtship. Before another month had passed, Sam was back at the Langdon mansion. Gradually, his charm and honest love won Livy's heart.

First, she only hinted at her love for Sam. Then she said that she truly loved him but was sorry she did and hoped it would soon pass. By the very next evening, she announced that she was proud and glad that she loved him!

Sam's heart nearly burst with joy. He wrote letters to his friends and family bragging about his success at last. But the triumph was short-lived. Nearly immediately, Sam discovered that he had a problem. In fact, he had two problems. The problems were Livy's mother and her father.

Both parents wanted to know a good deal more about him. Mrs. Langdon asked Sam for the names and addresses of eighteen people who knew him well enough to tell her more about his character and behavior. Mr. Langdon asked for six different names. While Mr. and Mrs. Langdon wrote letters to the people Sam had named, Sam returned to lecturing and writing love letters to Livy.

After a couple of months had passed, Jervis Langdon had collected the replies to his letters and sent for Sam. In a private meeting with Mr. Langdon, Sam listened to the awful news that the letters had brought. Most of the people not only disapproved of Sam, they seemed anxious to make a point of describing his bad character. A minister and a Sunday school teacher predicted that Sam would die a hopeless drunkard. In his *Autobiography*, Sam described what happened next:

"The reading of the letters finished, there was a good deal of a pause and it consisted largely of sadness .... I couldn't think of anything to say. Mr. Langdon was apparently in the same condition."

Finally, Mr. Langdon looked Sam directly in the eyes and said, "What kind of people are these? Haven't you a friend in the world?"

Sam did have some good friends, but he hadn't given their names to Livy's parents. He thought other people would give more honest opinions about him. To Mr. Langdon's question, he could only think to answer by saying, "Apparently not."

Sam could barely believe Mr. Langdon's next words. "I'll be your friend myself," he said kindly. "Take the girl. I know you better than they do."

Sam and Livy were engaged to be married. Still, one final problem remained. Sam needed enough money to support not only himself but to also help his mother, Pamela, and from time to time Orion and his family, as well as Livy. In less than a year, the problem was solved.

Sam wasn't sure how successful *The Innocents Abroad*

would be. His first book had been pretty much of a failure, selling only about 4,000 copies. But when the American Publishing Company brought out his second book, it was an incredible success. In the first year alone, more than 100,000 copies of *The Innocents Abroad* were sold at $3.50 each. Its earnings brought Sam as much as $1,500 a month, nearly a year's salary for the secretary of the territory of Nevada.

Economic problems behind him for the moment, Sam married his beloved Livy on February 2, 1870. At the age of thirty-four, Sam's days of high adventure were over. For a wedding gift, Livy's wealthy father gave the newlyweds a three-story brick house in a fancy neighborhood in Buffalo, New York.

Sam and Livy moved to Buffalo, where Sam had purchased an interest in a local newspaper. Although the pair did not stay long in Buffalo, Sam was settling into the ways he would follow for most of his mature years. These are the years when he would write the books that would make him famous the world over.

Chapter 6

FAME AND MISFORTUNE

The Innocents Abroad had been a smashing success. That one book had brought Sam to the attention of a world hungry for someone who could describe the things he saw with humor and an original point of view. But *The Innocents Abroad* was just the first rung of Sam's long climb to world-wide fame. During the next twenty years he settled down with Livy and wrote the most famous collection of books so far written by an American author.

Sam waited until relatively late in his life to be married. Nevertheless, after his marriage to Olivia he still had more than half of his life ahead of him. But his days of wandering throughout America and the world in search of adventure were over. Before his marriage, he had only wanted to travel and seek his fortune in the most exciting and exotic places he could imagine. But after he fell in love with Livy, he could only think of settling down, of living the life of a respected gentleman.

His adventurous youth was finished, but the mischievous glint of a young boy from Hannibal provided the power to nearly all the great books he was about to write. Livy had always noticed the child in Sam, even as a mature man. She affectionately called him "Youth" throughout their long and happy marriage. In the books that he wrote over the next several decades, Sam poured out his youthful experiences along the Mississippi River and in the West. No other American writer has cherished his youth so dearly.

Little more than a year after his marriage, Sam made a whirlwind trip around the country giving lectures to earn money. As Mark Twain, the author of *The Innocents Abroad,* Sam was popular enough to fill lecture halls wherever his schedule took him. When he arrived at Chicago, he saw the charred remains of the giant city that had burned to the scorched ground just two months before his visit. It was the largest fire disaster in American history.

On his lecture tour, Sam told some of the same stories that he had included in his third book, *Roughing It.* In just a few months, the book was due to be published by the American Publishing Company. In *Roughing It,* the man now known to the world as Mark Twain told about his adventures traveling to Nevada with Orion, his days as a prospector, and his trip to the Sandwich Islands. While he was still traveling, talking to packed houses throughout the nation, Livy wrote him a letter urging him to come home. He quickly did.

Just one month after *Roughing It* was published, Livy gave birth to the couple's first daughter. They named the baby Olivia Susan Clemens, but almost from the start they nicknamed her Susy. Both parents gave a healthy sigh of relief when they saw that Susy was robust and healthy. A year earlier, Livy had given birth to a son. Born several months too early, the baby boy was never strong or healthy and died the same year that Susy was born.

Like *The Innocents Abroad*, *Roughing It* was very successful right from the beginning. In the first four months after its publication, *Roughing It* sold more than sixty thousand copies. The next year, Sam published another book called *The Gilded Age*. Sam wrote the book with the help of a friend, a man named Charles Dudley Warner. The book was popular enough, but soon a lucky break came for Sam.

A writer who lived in Utah read *The Gilded Age* soon after it was published. The Western writer was so impressed by the book that he decided to write a play based upon it. The play was called *Colonel Sellers* and played in scores of theaters all over the country. The stage show was so popular that Sam earned more money from it than he did from the book that it was based on. From both the play and the book, Sam earned nearly $100,000.

Sam and his family were rich! Now that they had plenty of money, Livy was anxious for her family to have a permanent home. They had moved several times since their marriage. After talking about it for some time, Sam and Livy decided to hire people to build a house exactly the way they wanted. It was to be in Hartford, Connecticut, a town not far from New York City. While the house was being built, Sam took Livy and young Susy to Europe.

The year after the family moved into the Hartford house, Livy gave birth to her second daughter. The happy parents named her Clara Langdon Clemens. In the same year, Sam began work on one of his greatest masterpieces, a work for young people entitled *The Adventures of Tom Sawyer*. It was a book about Sam's own boyhood in Hannibal. In many ways, when Sam wrote about Tom Sawyer, a boy who seemed to always be getting into mischief, he was really writing about himself. Many of the adventures from Sam's early years are included in *The Adventures of Tom Sawyer*.

Sam worked on the book during the happiest years of his life. His two daughters were healthy and growing up strong. Livy, who had never been healthy, seemed to get stronger as she adjusted to family life. She even helped Sam edit the pages he wrote, and Sam constantly teased her about the work. With plenty of money, Sam had helped his mother, his sister Pamela, and Orion and his family move east to be closer to him.

Strangely, Sam wasn't sure that *The Adventures of Tom Sawyer* was a good enough book to publish. He found it hard to believe that the world would be interested in a book simply telling about his childhood in Hannibal. Wondering what to do, he showed his typed version of the book to a friend, a man named William Dean Howells. Mr. Howells was editor of *The Atlantic Monthly* magazine. He reassured Sam that the book told a fascinating tale and definitely deserved to be published. Over the years, *Tom Sawyer* became one of Sam's best-selling books, and an ideal introduction for young people to his works.

A year after *Tom Sawyer* was published, Alexander Graham Bell made his new invention, the telephone, available commercially. Hartford, Connecticut, became the first city in the world to install usable telephones. At first, Sam thought that the new invention was nothing but an interesting toy. But he quickly changed his mind. Less than a year later, Sam was one of the few people in the world using the telephone regularly. Of course, the new invention wasn't as sophisticated as it is today. With a wire strung from his house to the Western Union telegraph office in town, Sam could only call that one place.

The same year that he got his telephone, Sam decided to visit Europe again. He had been fascinated by the Old Country since his first visit there aboard the *Quaker City* years earlier. Now he traveled with Livy, Susy, Clara, and a family friend from Hartford. The travelers spent most of their time in Germany and France. While he was in Europe, Sam worked on two new books. The Clemens family stayed in Europe for a year and a half, not returning to Hartford until 1880.

The year 1880 was an important one for Sam. Returning to Hartford, he published a book called *A Tramp Abroad*, which had been partly based on his recent European trip. He also finished writing one of his most popular works, a book called *The Prince and the Pauper*. Even more important, that very same year Livy had her third daughter, who was named Jean.

Also in 1880, an important event of a different sort occurred. That year a man named Dwight Buell visited Sam in his house in Hartford. Mr. Buell was a local jeweler who, like everyone else, knew that Sam had made a lot of money from his popular books. Mr. Buell spoke to Sam about a new machine that was being built by an inventor named James W. Paige. James Paige was developing a typesetting machine.

In his youth, Sam had worked for years in Missouri and the East and West coasts setting type for newspapers by hand. He understood what a slow process it was to take tiny letters of the alphabet made of metal and position them in trays to be put on the printing press. The jeweler explained how Mr. Paige's machine would do the hard work automatically. Once the bugs were worked out, a person could use the machine to set the metal type almost as easily as he could use a typewriter.

Mr. Buell also explained that the new invention was not yet perfected and needed a bit more work. The inventor, Mr.

Paige, needed money so that he could continue testing and perfecting it. Sam was impressed by the incredible typesetting machine. He decided to give money to James Paige so that he could get the machine ready to be manufactured and sold to printers throughout the world.

While Paige was working on the new invention, Sam was working on a new book. A few years earlier, Sam had published a series of articles about his days as a riverboat pilot on the Mississippi River. The stories had been published in *The Atlantic Monthly*, the magazine edited by his friend William Dean Howells. Sam called the articles "Old Times on the Mississippi" because they described what the mighty river was like before the Civil War and the railroads had cut riverboat traffic to practically nothing.

Now Sam was anxious to make a book out of his magazine stories. For some time, he worked on the old articles, expanding and polishing them a bit to get them ready for the book. When it was published, he called it *Life on the Mississippi*. Some of the stories in chapter 3 of this book are from *Life on the Mississippi*.

When *Life on the Mississippi* was completed, Sam returned to a book he had been working on for years, but had put aside. The book was a novel about the boy Sam called Tom Sawyer and another boy he named Huckleberry Finn. The unfinished book told how Tom and Huck helped a runaway slave escape from the people who were searching for him and would certainly kill him if he were caught.

As it did in so many of Sam's books, the Mississippi River played an important role in the book Sam decided to call *The Adventures of Huckleberry Finn*. In it, Huck, Tom, and the slave named Jim escaped from the people looking for them by floating on a raft hundreds of miles down the Mississippi. Along the way, they met colorful characters and had strange adventures. More than any other book, *The Adventures of Huckleberry Finn* captured the magic of Sam's boyhood.

When he finally finished *Huckleberry Finn* in 1884, Sam decided to begin his own publishing company. The first book the new company published would be *The Adventures of Huckleberry Finn*. He decided to let a young man named Charles L. Webster run the new company. Charles Webster was his sister Pamela's son-in-law. Although Mr. Webster had no publishing experience, he had been helping Sam keep track of his finances for the last few years. And, of course, Sam always tried to help the people in his family.

When the Webster Publishing Company brought out *The Adventures of Huckleberry Finn*, it was an immediate, smashing success. Of all Sam's books, it sold the most copies when it first came out and earned the most money.

At the same time he had been finishing *Huckleberry Finn*, Sam was already thinking of the second book to be published by his company. For some years Sam had been trying to talk Ulysses S. Grant into writing a book about his life story. During the Civil War, Grant had been the most important general in the Union army. For eight years after the war, he was president of the United States.

After President Grant left office in 1877, he lost almost all his money in an investment swindle. By 1884, the year that Sam finished *The Adventures of Huckleberry Finn*, Grant was nearly penniless and was slowly dying from cancer in a hospital. Needing some way to support his wife, President Grant finally decided to write his life story and sell it.

Sam was angered when he heard the deals East Coast book publishers offered the ex-president. The 10 percent they offered Grant must have reminded him of the arrangements he had once had with the American Publishing Company. Sam offered to give President Grant 70 percent of the profits from his book if he would agree to publish it with the Webster Publishing Company. Grant agreed, and worked day and night to finish the long book. He dictated the final word just four days before he died.

Sam made a mighty effort to make the ex-president's book a success. He hired thousands of salesmen to travel the nation and get orders for the new book. By the hundreds of thousands, the orders poured in. When the book was ready to be printed, there were so many orders that twenty different printing presses were needed to keep up with the demand.

Grant's book sold more than 600,000 copies. The first payment to Grant's widow by the Webster Publishing Company was for $200,000. In all, she would receive more than twice that amount. In the history of the world, no author had received a single check for a book as large as the first check Mrs. Grant was given by Mark Twain's publishing company. As if that wasn't enough, Sam collected even more money so that the famous Grant's Tomb could be built in New York City.

These were the happiest years of Sam's life. Although his mother, brother, and sister had moved back to Iowa, he had Livy and his children to keep him company in the fancy Hartford house. And there was plenty of money coming in through the Webster Publishing Company so that Sam could help his relations in Iowa.

Sam worked on his books in the Hartford house and, often during the summers, at a farm owned by Livy's family near Elmira. Just as Livy had helped Sam edit and correct his earliest books, now his whole family got into the act. Writing in his *Autobiography*, Sam described the happy scene:

"The children always helped their mother to edit my books in manuscript. She would sit on the porch at the farm and read aloud, with her pencil in her hand, and the children would keep an alert and suspicious eye upon her right along, for the belief was well grounded in them that whenever she came across a particularly satisfactory passage she would strike it out."

Sam constantly teased Livy about her editing of his books. Sometimes he would write particularly bad sentences into the pages of his manuscript just to see if Livy would cross them out. When she did, Sam and the children would beg her to leave them in.

"It was three against one and most unfair," Sam wrote. "But it was very delightful and I could not resist the temptation. Now and then we gained the victory and there was much rejoicing. Then I privately struck the passage out myself. It had served its purpose."

The same year that the Webster Publishing Company had such success with President Grant's book, Susy Clemens decided to write a book about her famous father. At the age of fifteen, Susy was not a perfect speller, but when Livy found the book hidden in her room and showed it to Sam, he was pleased and proud beyond words. In her biography, Susy described her happy family and told about her father's habits, both good and not so good. She decided that he was a "*very* striking character." Sam decided that Susy was a "frank biographer and an honest one ...." The proud father put many passages from Susy's biography into his own *Autobiography*.

Undoubtedly, Sam would gladly have lived out his days in this happy situation, but it was not to be. Despite the vast amounts of money he had made from his famous books and lecture tours, Sam was spending freely. He had invested more than $150,000 into James Paige's typesetting machine, and it still wasn't ready to be marketed. He constantly sent money to his family in Iowa. To make matters worse, the Webster Publishing Company was not doing well since it had published its first two successful books. Always kind-hearted, Sam continued publishing unworthy books by friends who were down on their luck. The books lost a considerable amount of money.

Throughout the late 1880s, the publishing company continued to go downhill. Sam's financial picture did the same. It was helped somewhat in 1889 when Sam published one of his best-known books, *A Connecticut Yankee in King Arthur's Court*. But his debts were growing so heavy that even a successful book could not entirely wipe them out.

Then, in 1890, came even worse news. Jane Clemens, the wise and loving mother who had nursed Sam through his early years, had died in Keokuk. Through his sorrow, Sam remembered her in his *Autobiography*: "She had a slender, small body, but a large heart—a heart so large that everybody's grief and everybody's joys found welcome in it."

By the time his mother died, Sam was surrounded with money problems. The Webster Publishing Company continued to lose money. The Paige typesetting machine still wasn't ready to be marketed. Susy was starting college at an expensive university. Finally, in 1891, Sam decided that the family could live more cheaply in Europe than in America. Although she thought she would return, that year Livy shut the doors of her beloved Hartford house for the last time.

For years, the Clemens family traveled all over Europe, working on Sam's books and seeing the sights of the fascinating continent. But the news from America was bad. The country was going through another financial depression. In the bad business conditions, the Webster Publishing Company failed in April of 1894. When the company went bankrupt, it still owed nearly $100,000 to just under one hundred different people or companies.

While Livy waited in Paris, Sam traveled to New York where a bankruptcy court would decide how to best pay the people who had lost money with the Webster Publishing Company. Legally, Sam could have walked away from the company's debts. Even though it was his company, he had not personally taken on the bills the company owed. Even if he had, laws governing business in the United States would not have held Sam personally responsible for paying those bills, if his company could not.

But Sam regarded the fortune in past due bills as a matter of personal honor. He did not want to be involved in any way with a company that cheated people. He promised all the people who had lost money with the Webster Publishing Company that he would somehow repay them. Most people were happy to hear this.

In the past when Sam needed money, he had traveled around the United States giving lectures. Now, even though he was growing old, he decided that he would do it again. But this time he would travel throughout the world to earn as much money as he possibly could.

Livy couldn't stand the thought of staying behind while Sam was gone for a year or more. Sam and Livy decided to travel together. And they would bring Clara along as a secretary. Susy and Jean would stay behind. Sam, Livy, and Clara began the endless trip on July 14, 1895. Half the world wished Sam well as he began the mighty effort of repaying his company's debts. Everyone knew what a challenge he was facing.

Sam traveled by train westward across the United States. Everywhere he stopped, he spoke to huge crowds in halls and theaters sold out weeks in advance. On the way west, he also stopped in some cities in Canada. Everywhere he went, he was greeted by kind strangers who wished him well, and felt they knew him from his books. When he finally arrived in San Francisco, so many people wanted to see their old hero that he had to give nine different lectures in that one city alone.

Even when he had reached San Francisco and the Pacific Ocean, the westward journey was just beginning. The three Clemenses boarded the oceangoing *Warramoo* and continued west. Of all the stops on the long trip, Sam was most anxious to see the Sandwich Islands once again. But when the *Warramoo* reached Honolulu harbor, no one was allowed to leave the ship. An epidemic of cholera had broken out on the island and no passengers were to go ashore. Sam was bitterly disappointed.

Then it was on to Australia, New Zealand, and India. Even in faraway India, where people knew little about America or Americans, they knew about Mark Twain. Throughout his travels, no hall or auditorium was large enough to hold all the people who wanted to hear the famous American writer speak. The roar of the crowds everywhere made Sam feel almost young again. From every port, he sent money back to the United States to help pay off the Webster Publishing Company's debts.

A year and a day after he had left Elmira to begin the long tour, Sam gave his final lecture in South Africa and headed back for his rented home in England. It had been a triumphant tour! Much of the great debt had already been repaid. Now Sam looked forward to bringing his whole family back together again. All were scheduled to come together in the rented house in England.

Sam, Livy, and Clara arrived in England on July 31, 1896. Susy and Jean were due to arrive shortly. But a week went by and they didn't come. Instead, a letter came saying that Susy was ill but would be along soon. Although the tone of the letter was optimistic, Sam was worried. He rushed to a telegraph office in England and sent a cable to the United States asking for more infromation about Susy's condition. The only reply he got said: "Wait for cablegram in the morning."

The cablegram that came the next morning was frightening. It said that Susy's illness would require a long period of recovery. Livy and Clara boarded the first ship bound for America. They would return to the Hartford house, where Susy had been taken to rest, and care for her until she was well. Sam would stay behind in England to find a larger house where Susy could rest as soon as she was well enough to travel to England.

Livy and Clara were still on the high seas when, three days later, Sam was handed a cablegram. Sam read the words in shock and disbelief. Susy had died from meningitis, a serious infectious disease. She was twenty-four years old.

Sam's grief knew no bounds. His beloved Susy, his playful biographer and biggest fan, his favorite daughter in a home of favorites, was dead. And then he thought of Livy. She would travel to the Hartford house and discover the awful news. To soften the blow, if such was possible, Sam sent his wife urgent letters so that he could break the news to her gently.

For more than five years the Clemenses roamed throughout Europe trying to escape the sorrow that no one can run away from. Sam published a book about his world lecture tour called *Following the Equator*. It earned quite a bit of money and was used to pay off the Webster Publishing Company debts.

Finally, near the start of 1898, Sam finished paying off all his debts. It had taken four years of hard work and saving to do it, but newspapers around the world printed the headlines stating that Mark Twain had paid all the debts of his publishing company. Every penny.

Finally free of the terrible debt, Sam and Livy decided that they had enough money to return to the United States. They returned to New York on October 15, 1900. No European king and queen could have had a grander reception. Newspapers across the nation told of the return of Mark Twain in front-page headlines.

Sam and Livy still had a few more good years ahead of them, Sam a few more than Livy. Although the nation sang the praises of its most famous writer, there had been great sadness in his life, and there would yet be more. But there was also laughter. Anyone who touched the heart and mind of Mark Twain would live far longer than anyone could suppose. His family and friends are alive everywhere in the wonderful books of Mark Twain. Reading about their joys and sorrows, you can almost see the twinkle in the eye of a young boy from Hannibal, Missouri.

Mark Twain 1835-1910

1835 Unsuccessful attempt to assassinate President Jackson. Halley's Comet seen.

1837 Economic depression begins. Victoria becomes queen in England.

1841 President Harrison dies one month after inauguration.

1844 Morse sends first telegraph message, "What hath God wrought!"

1851 *Uncle Tom's Cabin* published by Harriet Beecher Stowe.

1856 Abolitionist John Brown and his forces murder pro-slavery settlers at Pottawatomie Creek in Kansas.

1857 Dred Scott Decision by U.S. Supreme Court—Negro slave is found to be still a slave even if living in free territory.

1859 Abolitionist John Brown is hanged after he tries to start a slave revolt. Darwin publishes *Origin of Species*.

1860 Abraham Lincoln elected president. South Carolina secedes.

1861 Civil War begins. Tsar Alexander II frees Russian serfs. Kingdom of Italy is born; Victor Emmanuel is king.

1863 Lincoln issues Emancipation Proclaimation, which frees slaves in Confederate states. Samuel Langhorne Clemens adopts the pen name Mark Twain.

1865 Civil War ends. Lincoln assassinated.

1869 Mark Twain publishes *The Innocents Abroad*. Suez Canal opens.

1876 Battle of Little Bighorn; General Custer defeated by Sioux and Cheyenne. Twain publishes *The Adventures of Tom Sawyer*. Queen Victoria becomes Empress of India.

1877 Reconstruction ends in South. Twain and Bret Harte write *Ah Sin*, a play.

1881 President Garfield is assassinated in Washington, D.C. Twain publishes *The Prince and the Pauper*. Alexander II of Russia is assassinated.

1883 Twain publishes *Life on the Mississippi*.

1884 Ottmer Mergenthaler patents the Linotype machine, a typesetting machine that casts one line at a time. Twain publishes *The Adventures of Huckleberry Finn*.

1886 Statue of Liberty dedicated in New York Harbor.

1889 Twain publishes *A Connecticut Yankee in King Arthur's Court*.

1893 Economic depression begins. Sigmund Freud and Josef Breuer publish their theories on psychoanalysis in Austria.

1894 Twain publishes *Tom Sawyer Abroad* and *The Tragedy of Pudd'nhead Wilson*. First Sunday comics appear. Last tsar of Russia, Nicholas II, takes the throne.

1896 First moving picture shown in public in New York City.

1901 President McKinley is assassinated. Queen Victoria of England dies; Edward VII becomes king.

1903 Orville and Wilbur Wright make first successful airplane flight.

1907 Fall of the stock market.

1908 Model T introduced on the market. America's first skyscraper completed.

1909 Robert Peary and company are first to reach the North Pole.

1910 Halley's Comet is seen. George V becomes king of England.

127

ABOUT THE AUTHOR

Jim Hargrove has worked as a writer and editor for more than 10 years. After serving as an editorial director for three Chicago area publishers, he began a career as an independent writer, preparing a series of books for children. He has contributed to works by nearly 20 different publishers. With his wife and 13-year-old daughter, he lives in a small Illinois town near the Wisconsin border.